REMARKABLE COURAGE

TAG Publishing, LLC
2618 S. Lipscomb
Amarillo, TX 79109
www.TAGPublishers.com

Office (806) 373-0114
Fax (806) 373-4004
info@TAGPublishers.com

ISBN: 9781934606421

Cover: Lloyd Arbour, www.tablloyd.com
Text: Lloyd Arbour, www.tablloyd.com

First Edition

Copyright © 2013 Deb Cheslow

All rights reserved. No part of this book may be reproduced in any form without prior written permission from the publisher. The opinions and conclusions draw in this book are solely those of the author. The author and the publisher bear no liability in connection with the use of the ideas presented.

REMARKABLE COURAGE

A SYSTEMIZED STRATEGY FOR SUCCESS

DEB CHESLOW

Table of Contents

Acknowledgements 7
Preface 9
Pre-Flight 11
Mission Briefing 29
Aim High 43
Basic Training 55
What's Holding You Back 79
Autopilot Engaged 97
Maneuvering Through The Storm 113
No Pain, No Gain: How Bad Do You Want It? 133
Flight Planning Secrets 149
Aim, <u>Fire</u>, Ready 163
Fly – Fight – Win 177
About The Author 195
About Deb Cheslow Consulting 197

ACKNOWLEDGEMENTS

I am filled with gratitude for all who contributed to this book. It would not have been possible without the collaborative efforts of so many people.

First and foremost, I extend heartfelt gratitude to my partner and best friend, Angie Flynn, who pours her heart and soul into everything she does. Without you, I would never have found the courage to put these words in print.

To our amazing children – Erin, Nicki and Josh. Enduring the creation of two books in one year is a lot to ask. Thank you for your patience and understanding. I love you all!

To my other children – Mylif and Pooka (most people would call them dogs) for always being there with a kiss and a snuggle.

To Deb Cheslow Consulting's Executive Marketing Director, Freddie Smith. Thanks for helping me "get over myself" and share your vision with the world.

To our publisher, Dee Burks, at TAG Publishing. Thanks for being such an amazing person to work with. We look forward to working with you for a long time to come!

Again, to my daughter (and our editor), Erin Cheslow. Thank you for the wonderful editing job you performed on this manuscript. I'm an engineer, not a grammarian.

To my parents, Charles and Jean Myers. Thanks for always being there for me and supporting me even when you didn't agree with my decisions. All I am today is because of your example.

To the Virginia Tech Corps of Cadets (B'87) for exemplifying the power of discipline, accountability, standards and systems in achieving remarkable success. I would not be where I am today without you all.

Ut Prosim! Go Guard!

PREFACE By Tom Feltenstein

> "Discipline takes courage – but where would your life be if every time you said 'I should...,' you actually DID?"
>
> –DEB CHESLOW

It is such a pleasure to introduce you to *Remarkable Courage* and Deb Cheslow. Deb Cheslow is one of those rare individuals who looks right past obstacles – she relentlessly pursues her goals and refuses to allow people or circumstances to sway her decisions or move her off her path.

Finally someone has written an honest and perceptive book on the topic of success that shares a systemized strategy for creating extraordinary results – in business and in everyday life. This book is fascinating! It lays out the four key, foundational pillars that are essential to success in any venture – discipline, accountability, standards and systems. Deb then goes further to provide the tools

necessary for building on these pillars to create whatever success you dare to dream.

This is an exceptional story - a treasure trove of information, and a "one of a kind" perspective on the subject of creating success. *Remarkable Courage* is a refreshing, one-stop shop resource, with tangible tools that will enable anyone to accomplish their goals and live out their dreams. Deb constructs a framework where the reader discovers the courage to put logic aside and reach for larger than life dreams and meet with extraordinary success. I'm not talking about incremental progress here, I'm talking about true quantum leaps!

It is important to study this book as a process so you can truly experience the unprecedented transformation that takes place.

PRE-FLIGHT

When I was approached about writing this book I was, quite honestly, dumbfounded. What did I have to say on the topic of living a *"courageous"* life, much less a "remarkably courageous" life? I have lived a *good* life... a *successful* life ... a *fun* life. I have helped people and companies all over the world do the same. I have been driven all my life seemingly by some unseen force to be the best at whatever I attempt to do – I have a desire – no, a NEED to accomplish things that most people would perceive as impossible; but courageous? I wasn't so sure. There are so many times that I have just been scared to death, nearly paralyzed by fear – where's the courage in that? But then it was pointed out to me that courage isn't the absence of fear; rather, it's feeling the fear and then stepping into action in spite of that fear. Cast in that light, yes, I believe I have a good bit to say on the subject of acting in spite of fear and if that is "courageous," then yes, I have absolutely lived a courageous life.

My question to you is: Do YOU have the courage to pursue and achieve goals that seem absolutely outrageous in your business and your life? I don't care what all the self-help books and gurus

tell you, it takes a lot more than a dream and a wish to make it happen! You will run into dead ends and brick walls and nay-sayers and other obstacles that you can't even imagine on your journey. Do you have the courage, the fortitude, the persistence and the desire to pick yourself up, dust yourself off and keep pressing forward – even when it all seems hopeless? Because that is what it takes!

It also takes belief – belief in your mission and belief that you can achieve it and that you deserve it. That seems rather simple, doesn't it? Yet, building your belief is often the hardest part of the process. That being said, it's also the best part – it IS a process and that is what *Remarkable Courage* is all about – the process of defying logic and turning an unrealistic vision into reality. I have done it over and over and over again in my life and in my business and it is my privilege to share this information with you.

This information will not make your brain hurt – it doesn't take rocket science to make it work. The process is incredibly simple – so simple, in fact that most people really overcomplicate it or dismiss it out of hand as just so much "fluff." It is simple, though not necessarily easy; but then, I never said it was going to be easy – only worth it!

Within the pages of *Remarkable Courage* I use the foundational principles that are integral to military success and lay them out in a systemized methodology that can be duplicated in the corporate arena to take any company, organization or team to the next level. This strategy is rooted in four broad areas of core competency that, I contend, too many corporations have strayed from: Standards, Discipline, Accountability and Systems. I present the theory, show you the steps you need to take to apply the theory in the real world, offer examples from my own experiences of how I have made the process work in my own career and life, and then I give you the tools you need to keep the snowball building long after you have finished the book and put it on your bookshelf (which I really hope you won't do – this is one of those books you really need to keep coming back to so you can refresh yourself on the basics over and over again – something to keep in mind as you begin your journey).

Before I get into everything, let me tell you a little bit about myself. I believe that before you can truly understand where a person is coming from, you have to know a bit about where they CAME from. I want you to see that I'm just a regular person – there is nothing terribly remarkable about my life, even though I have done remarkable things.

I wasn't born with a silver spoon in my mouth or with a hefty trust fund or rich, well-connected relatives in high places. I was born, Deborah Jane Myers, into a wonderful family on February 6, 1965. My parents were very middle class – my father owned a sheet metal construction company in Baltimore, MD and my mother was a stay-at-home mom for my younger brother and me. They were amazing role models!! They both lived their passion and jumped out of bed each day to "go to work," thoroughly enjoying their roles in life. Through their example, I learned several principles very early on that were ingrained into my core:

If you make a commitment (even if you don't necessarily like what you have committed to), you follow through;

Make decisions – you will never have all the information you need to make a perfect decision, so make decisions where you are with what you have; and

ANYTHING is possible, but you have to take action – you can't just wait for things to be handed to you in life.

It's only fairly recently that I have realized that not all parents are like mine. As I was growing up, my parents put absolutely no ceiling on the level to which I could or should aspire to achieve. They allowed me the freedom to explore my interests and develop my talents, and they NEVER encouraged me to have a Plan B, to be cautious, to protect myself or to avoid risk. As a result, I relentlessly pursued my passions in life and never allowed people or circumstances to sway me. The phrase "failure is not an option" is used as a cliché by many people; however, it was truly the motto I lived by growing up. I never even considered what might happen if I failed at something, and I never entertained the possibility of quitting anything. Now, that doesn't mean that the path to what I wanted was always easy or that I always got what I wanted exactly when I wanted it, but I was doggedly determined and passionately persistent in the pursuit of my goals.

I have always been attracted to structure and discipline. I suppose that is one of the reasons I did well in sports, earning 11 varsity letters in high school, and why I got straight A's throughout my high school career and why I was Valedictorian of my graduating class. It didn't necessarily come easy or naturally to me, but I was incredibly disciplined about practice and studying and was willing to do the work. I was teachable and I reaped the rewards of that structure I placed in my life.

As an early example, when I was a freshman in high school I really, REALLY wanted to play on the junior varsity (JV) basketball team. I loved basketball! I was always shooting baskets with my friends in the driveway, even though I had never actually played on a team before. My friend that I shot hoops with was much better than I was – she had played on recreation league teams before. We decided to try out for the JV team, and as the time for the try-outs neared, I found myself afraid that my friend would make the team and I might not – she was better than me – no doubt about it - and if a choice had to be made, surely the coaches would choose her.

The day after try-outs, the rosters were posted outside the gym. I eagerly searched the list of names, but as I feared, only her name was on the JV team roster. I was crushed. As I started to walk away to class, someone called me back – "Hey Debbie, here's your name over here!" I hadn't made the JV team – I had made the VARSITY team – as a freshman. It was unheard of! My freshman year I rode the bench, only playing when we were so far ahead of the other team that there was no risk at all in letting me play; however, by my senior year, I was the team captain and starting point guard.

At one point I actually asked my coach why on earth she picked me for the varsity team, and she told me that although I was raw, she saw potential – I was obviously coachable - and that, because I had never played on a team before, I didn't have any bad habits to break. Interesting... I was never a gifted athlete; I just loved the sport. I had a good attitude, the drive and determination to improve every single day and I was 100% coachable. The moral of the story is that you don't need huge talent and extraordinary ability to succeed. That's not what this book is about. Every person, team, and organization has the ability to be wildly successful.

When I got to college I met a lot of other people who were also valedictorians in high school, but many of them didn't even graduate college because they had little discipline, no systems in place and they didn't hold themselves accountable. They flunked out of college because they didn't know how to study and work hard.

Throughout my teenage years, as I was formulating the answer to the "What do you want to be when you grow up?" question, I knew two things: First and foremost, I wanted to be a wife and a mother. Second, I was not going to be content to wait around for "Mr. Right" to show up – I wanted to have a meaningful, exciting career – preferably utilizing math and airplanes – in the meantime. I wanted to pilot the Space Shuttle!

When the time came to decide on a college, I pretty much had my pick. MIT recruited me heavily, but I was uninterested in living in a northeastern city – the MIT lifestyle was just not for me. I was very drawn to the military – specifically the Air Force – so I looked at the Air Force Academy in Colorado Springs. I still remember the informational package coming in the mail. I sat down on my bed and tore the package open and started reading the glossy recruiting brochure. One sentence stood out in bold relief on the first page: "First and foremost, the mission of the U.S. Air Force Academy is to prepare cadets to be officers in the United States military. Your major and your career are secondary to that mission." The heck with that! I wanted to be an astronaut! My role as an Air Force officer was absolutely secondary to that goal – at least in my mind at the time. Ironically, once I joined the Corps of Cadets at Virginia Tech, my major absolutely took a back seat to my military career. I closed the brochure, put it in the trash and disqualified the Air Force Academy from my college selection process. After a campus visit, I decided to attend Virginia Polytechnic Institute and State University (Virginia Tech). The campus was gorgeous, the town was quaint and the university had a top 10 engineering college and offered a major in Aerospace (and Ocean) Engineering. I knew I would *never* be an engineer in real life – I could never be happy sitting behind a desk day after day designing some small piece of some subassembly that went into the wiring harness of something else that eventually went inside an airplane. I wanted adventure and excitement, but by majoring in Aerospace Engineering I could spend four years studying math and airplanes – it was a means to an end.

During my orientation visit a man in a uniform gave a presentation about the Corps of Cadets at Virginia Tech. I was star struck!! It was like love at first sight. With every fiber of my being, I KNEW the Corps of Cadets was where I wanted to spend my four years at Virginia Tech. My parents weren't too crazy about the idea, but they saw the look in my eyes, asked me if I was sure and then – as they had done my entire life – steadfastly supported my decision. I enrolled in the Corps that day.

I knew nothing about what was awaiting me during my first year in the VTCC – just what the brochures told me about honor and tradition and camaraderie. As I waved goodbye to my parents after moving into my dormitory, my roommate (who was a local) and I headed downtown, and she proceeded to tell me what being a freshman in the Corps meant and what was waiting for us. I was terrified!! We went back to the dorms, the last parents left, the doors closed and then all hell broke loose! Upperclassmen yelling 2 inches from your face, rules, rules, and more rules – even when you did things perfectly there was someone there yelling at you for doing it too well.

The mission of the "new cadet" (calling us "rats" was frowned upon as politically incorrect, although it happened anyway – tradition is hard to break) year is all about breaking you down – your pride, your ego, your habits – and building you back up with new habits that serve the unit. It is an object lesson in changing

paradigms (which we'll get into later). The military is masterful at using spaced repetition and emotional impact to change habits. Above all it teaches you to face fear and act in spite of that fear – the military programs its members with courage!

Many of my classmates chose to leave the university rather than endure the harsh treatment that pervaded the life of the freshman cadets. Now, Hollywood uses a lot of dramatic license, but if you have ever seen *Stripes*, *An Officer and A Gentleman* or *G.I. Jane*, you have an idea of what kind of stuff I'm talking about. Today, I imagine the powers that be would call it "hazing," but for us it was just part of the Corps – break you down so they can build you into what they wanted. I can't say I "enjoyed" how I was treated during this time, but there was no way I was going to quit. It was just a matter of making it through the year. Daily life was tough, but we were in no danger – nothing bad was going to happen to us. All we had to do was study hard, follow orders, make good grades and persist, and at the end of the year it would be over and we would be welcomed into the Corps as full-fledged members. So persistence was the name of the game – scream out the "Ma'ams" and "Sirs," keep my shoes shined, my uniform pressed, my nose clean and my grades high!

And I did. So well in fact that at the end of my first semester I had a 3.94 GPA and was offered a 3-1/2 year Air Force scholarship. Now, at the time, there were general scholarships (which essentially meant you would be an officer in your field when you graduated – an engineer, in my case) and there were PILOT scholarships. The Air Force wanted me as an engineer, but I had a burning desire to be a pilot. If I accepted the scholarship, I was bound to the US government for 4 years whether I became a pilot or not and whether I even graduated or not.

My parents did not want me to accept the scholarship – money was not an issue and they were happy to pay for my education and they did not like the idea of me being obligated to the military for four years after I graduated. But, although I knew they COULD pay for my education, why SHOULD they if I was being offered a means to reach my goals AND get my college tab picked up in the process? It was a small way I could give my parents something back for everything they had done for me. My mind was made up and again, although they didn't like it, they supported my decision.

I accepted the scholarship because I KNEW that I would be a pilot –which was absolutely illogical! There were no pilot scholarships readily available, and even if there were, they were incredibly competitive, they rarely gave them to women, and I had undergone eye surgery as a young child, which could prevent me from becoming a pilot at any rate. The only way I could get one of those scholarships was to earn either the Commandant's Award or the Vice-Commandant's Award at Field Training in between my sophomore and junior years. If I could get one of those awards I could convert my scholarship to a pilot scholarship. Again, a seemingly impossible, illogical task, but failure was not an option. I worked hard at field training, beat the odds and earned a Vice-Commandant's Award! I received my pilot's scholarship and graduated as the first female Air Force pilot from Virginia Tech and made it into their history books. Against all odds, I was headed for pilot training as a 2nd Lieutenant in the United States Air Force.

I absolutely loved my career in the Air Force, but it was not easy; there were seemingly insurmountable obstacles every step of the way. Again, persistence, determination, discipline, accountability and holding myself to a higher standard were the name of the game.

In fact I was told during the first week of training that I would likely wash out before ever setting foot in a jet (because I had an engineering degree and a high percentage of engineering majors never made it through), but I graduated near the top of my class at Pilot Training and was given my choice of assignments. There were a lot of sexy, glory-bound career tracks I could have chosen, but when all was said and done, I chose to become an Instructor Pilot – to teach other airmen to fly supersonic jets. I jumped out of bed every morning to go to "work." Wearing a flight suit was like wearing pajamas to the office and then I got to jump in a jet and fly all day. Plus, every couple of weeks money showed up in my bank account. What a life!

That's not to say it was all sunshine and lollipops, because it wasn't. I was responsible for deciding whether an airman was allowed the privilege of becoming a full-fledged pilot in the United States Air Force or not. The last thing I wanted to do was wash a student out. They trained with me for months and I got to know them – their hopes and dreams – I cared about them. But as their instructor, it was my job to put any emotions aside and look at the big picture: Fail him and he goes on to do other things with his life no matter how hurt or angry he may be in the moment; pass him and he goes on to be a pilot who makes a mistake and gets killed (you don't always get a second chance). There were tough decisions to be made each and every day. Through it all I had to keep the vision of my organization (the USAF) constantly in mind – developing Airmen to ensure an effective, mission ready Air Force. It's no different than running a company or an organization – you have to keep the big vision in mind and be willing and able to make hard decisions; you must have standards.

As my career progressed, so did my responsibilities. I moved from instructing pilots to instructing other instructors and then to evaluating other instructors. I loved every step of it. Along the way I met and married the man of my dreams and we started a family. While pregnant with our first child, I reached a tough decision point in my life and my career. My husband, Mark, was also an instructor pilot, but he was a year behind me in terms of seniority and assignments. The next step on my journey to astronaut was Test Pilot school, which would require us to split up our family for at least a year. This was not an acceptable option for me. I was being heavily recruited by the Air Force Academy as a Deputy Air Officer Commanding over one of the cadet squadrons. I was a female instructor pilot and a Captain – the perfect role model for the female cadets – and they wanted me badly! I was able to strike a deal (which is unusual) – I would take the assignment if they would also create a flying position for my husband and reassign him as well. The powers that be at Air Training Command (ATC) agreed and off we went to teach at the United States Air Force Academy.

It was a sacrifice on some levels for both of us – I was choosing my family over pursuing my path to astronaut, and we were both giving up piloting supersonic jets to instruct in a T-41 (a souped up Cessna) – kind of like trading in your V8 convertible for a bicycle. But we were together and we were happy – life was good!!

I attribute a great deal of my success in life to my focus on my vision. My Air Force career was flying high as a female instructor pilot with a prestigious special duty assignment at the Academy, but, with the arrival of our daughter, it became clear to both my husband and I that we didn't want our children raised by a nanny or a day care center. We quickly started entertaining the idea that one of us should leave the Air Force. In actuality, our first thought was that HE should leave the military. Fighter pilot slots were opening up to women and I could continue my string of "firsts" if I stayed. However, just like in business, things changed – politics changed, commanders changed, policies changed. Doors that were once wide open to me suddenly swung closed because I lacked operational experience. Unreasonable demands were placed on me regarding my assignment. The Air Force was restructuring so my contract (and my husband's contract) at the Academy was at the pleasure of new commanders who felt I needed to get "out in the field."

The best of my options was to relocate to Tinker AFB in Oklahoma and pilot an AWACS "spy" plane, but I would have to go alone. I was told that IF another AWACS slot opened up the following year, my husband may be able to get that assignment and join me. In my mind that was an unworkable situation for our family. I would be on assignment for 270 days each year and even if my husband was assigned to the same base, he would be gone a "different" 270 days. The overlap would mean that there would be a significant amount of time each year when our children (I was now pregnant with baby #2) would be without EITHER of us at home. It was unacceptable. I decided at that moment that my military career was over – my family was much more important to me than being a pilot in the Air Force. That doesn't mean it was an easy decision, but my vision was always in the forefront of my mind – and my overarching goal from the beginning was to have a family. What kind of life would any of us have if we were apart from each other for months and months at a time?

So I separated from the Air Force, but I didn't just quit pursuing goals and sit at home playing Barbies all day – I became a civilian flight instructor and worked around my husband's schedule. Several years later, my husband also separated from the Air Force. We moved to Virginia and built our dream house. Mark's dream was to become an airline pilot and he was hired by a commuter airline, which meant he was away from home several days each week. By this time both of my daughters were in school and I needed something to occupy my time, so I "created" a position as a part-time estimator at a construction company in town. It was a fun job because I got to play with math and computers while my girls were in school.

At this point something started to shift in my life. I had always been a goal achiever, but now I wasn't pursuing anything. I had everything I ever thought I wanted in my life – a great husband, two beautiful daughters, a fantastic house, cars, money was no problem – my life was "perfect," and yet I couldn't help but wonder "Is this all there is?" I now know what was happening, but at the time I just felt like a spoiled brat who was incapable of appreciating all the good in my life. At one point my husband actually looked at me and asked: "What's it going to take to make you happy, Deb? Look around you! What more do you want?" That was the question, wasn't it? What more DID I want? I didn't know, but what I did know was that something was missing. I was suddenly terrified that I would lose everything.

And then in 2002, the unthinkable happened. Mark and I were making Christmas cookies in the kitchen, watching our girls play in the snow when he told me that he wanted a divorce. He was in love with someone else and was leaving me, our children and our life together. No amount of pleading or begging would change his mind. Our idyllic 11 year marriage was over – poof! Ten days later, he was gone, and I thought my life was over.

Suddenly, I was forced to move into a full-time position at work in order to meet my financial obligations. I was miserable, but I was still a goal achiever at heart, so it wasn't long before I had completely systemized my job and there was absolutely no challenge to the work whatsoever. I was not happy, personally or professionally. I spent the better part of the next eight years throwing the grandest pity party the world has ever known.

With the same determination I had used to build my life, I subconsciously destroyed it. I put up walls of security around me that only a very few people were allowed to penetrate – I was determined that NO ONE would ever hurt me again. In retrospect it is clear that my depression seeped into every corner of my world – it was a palpable entity that affected me, my children, my friends, my job – everything. It also manifested itself in the health of my body – I was sick all the time and on numerous medications.

What the hell was wrong with me? What happened to the woman flying 600+ mph in formation three feet away from another aircraft – that cocky, self-assured spitfire who dared to dream the most audacious dreams imaginable and then go make them her reality? What had I become? The only thing that kept me going was my girls, who I loved above all else. I lived for those kids – spending large chunks of time volunteering at their school, flexing my work schedule around their school day and activities. They were my reason for getting out of bed each morning and continuing on each day. Essentially, I held myself accountable to them, but it wasn't enough.

One day it struck me that perhaps I needed something for myself too. I had wanted to study karate since I was 8 years old so at age 38 I finally decided to start taking classes. The study of Chinese Kempo Karate became my passion – the classes were the highlight of my days. My daughters also enrolled at the school, so it was something of a family affair. At age 42 I received my black belt. I taught at most of the children's classes and ran the conditioning program for the adults. I practically lived at the karate school when I wasn't at work.

Meanwhile, I became more and more disillusioned with my job and decided to strike out on my own. The burning desire to accomplish things was starting to come alive again. I formed my own consulting company and within a couple of months was managing Virginia's premier "green" building program for the western half of the state. It was about this time when I picked up the book "Think and Grow Rich" by Napoleon Hill. I was skeptical at first, but as I delved further into the book and began to actually study the concepts, I began to wonder, "What if..." Then I started applying the principles that the book espoused with focus and purpose and my life took off again like a rocket!!

With each passing week, I could feel myself changing. I was able to stop every medication that I was taking. I felt more physically and emotionally fit than I had in years – and the only thing that was different was my mindset! I used what I was learning to take stock of my life and figure out what my purpose on this earth was. The common thread through my entire life had been a sincere love and desire to teach, coach, and train people and a thought kept nagging in the back of my mind that I could combine that love with my business.

I drew upon every ounce of courage I possessed to make the decision to completely retool my business. My green building consulting business was doing well and I had a steady income, but it was never going to afford me the lifestyle I desired. Logically, it was

not the time to be making any drastic changes to the business. The economy was a mess – in the middle of the worst recession of my lifetime – and changing business directions was a risky decision at best – at worst it was professional suicide. Still, even though it didn't make logical sense, I boldly shut down my green building business and started working with individuals and businesses to help them change the results they were getting.

A year later I made the decision to relocate my growing business and my family from Virginia to Florida – a whole new set of opportunities and possibilities disguised as obstacles and challenges popped up, but it turned out to be the best move I could have made. I won't kid you though, I was scared to death – it took every ounce of courage I could muster to follow through with the move.

It is interesting to look back and see with crystal clarity that I created my life by holding onto a vision and courageously stepping into action all along the path. When my husband left our marriage, I used all the same tools I had employed to create all the good in my life to destroy it – to destroy my happiness, my health, my peace of mind. Then I discovered my purpose and was able to reignite the engines of creation to propel my life to even greater heights of achievement.

I have taken the strategies and methods I have used throughout my life to create the results that I wanted – tools that I honed to a razor sharp edge in the Air Force – the high standards, the discipline, the accountability and the systems – and distilled them into a duplicable process that works for individuals, teams, organizations and companies, to help them make quantum leap improvements in their performance and reach goals that otherwise seem impossible. That's what I teach in my private consulting practice, in my speaking business and in my books and programs, and that's what I'm excited to share with you now. So strap on your parachute, fasten your seatbelt and hold on for the ride. With this book you are going to find the courage to take massive actions that lead to massive results at supersonic speeds!

REMARKABLE COURAGE

1 | MISSION BRIEFING

There is no doubt in my mind that I was destined to be in the military – I was born with all the raw material that makes for good soldiers, sailors, airmen and marines. I have always craved discipline and structure and I seem to innately systemize everything. These characteristics were honed to a razor sharp edge, both in the Virginia Tech Corps of Cadets, and in the Air Force; however, once I left the military and started working in industry, I was dumbfounded! How did the U.S. economy continue to prosper when corporate America operated so haphazardly?

Military units function efficiently and purposefully – they know what the mission is, and they get the job done quickly and effectively. Every person in the unit knows what their function is and what they are expected to do to move the unit closer to the mission objective. Of course, that doesn't mean that things always turn out exactly right, but there is purposeful action every step of the way. On the other hand, the private sector tends to move so slowly, with so much bureaucracy and so many layers of authority, it's a wonder anything gets done! As a product of Air Force training, it was only natural that, as I started my own company, I would fall back on that experience. From Day 1, I relied on discipline, accountability and standards to direct my operations and then glued it all together with systems to ensure consistent results. I was excited by how productive our operations were and how quickly we met our objectives.

It has been my privilege to get a behind the scenes look at numerous corporate and organizational operations, large and small, and I have concluded that one of the main reasons why 95% of new businesses fail within the first five years and why so many companies and organizations struggle is because they have lost sight of the four main pillars of success: Discipline, accountability, standards and systems. Companies and individuals alike also seem to have forgotten that they – and only they – are responsible for their results. Blaming outside forces for, complaining about or justifying lackluster results are a neon sign pointing to the fact that you are not taking responsibility for your results. Until you do, your four pillars will be built on sand and will never help you build what you want.

With the proper strategies, tactics and tools to build upon this four-pillar foundation you can create whatever level of success you choose, for your business and for your life.

DISCIPLINE

Discipline is centered around following commands. At its most basic level it is giving *yourself* a command and then following it, come what may. It's not enough to wish for things or hope that circumstances turn out the way you want. You have to decide what you want, commit to the decision and then have the discipline to do whatever it takes to follow through. See, I believe that most company management teams do a fair job of deciding what they want – they set objectives for various metrics within the organization – sales goals, profitability goals, safety goals, quality goals, etc. – and they do a decent job of committing to them and articulating the goals to the rest of the company employees. Where they fall short is in instilling the discipline – both in themselves and their employees – to meet those objectives come what may.

Discipline takes courage – it is not comfortable or easy to do whatever it takes. Let's face it, you can preach the party line at your employees all day long, but just like children, they are going to do what you do – not what you say. So you can't expect your staff to be disciplined if you, as their leader, are not. Think about the qualities that you most need in your employees in order to meet your objectives and then get real with yourself, do a personal inventory and see if you possess those same qualities. Then keep reading; this book is going to show you everything you need to know to change whatever habits need changing (regardless of the nature of the habit).

Your results don't lie. If you are not getting the results you want, it is simply because you are not acting in ways that are consistent with those results. Make no mistake, discipline is a habit and it can be cultivated just as surely as you can develop the habit of brushing your teeth. The entire process is in the pages of this book.

In the spring of my senior year in high school I was riding high. I would be off to Virginia Tech in the Fall as a member of the Corps of Cadets and Air Force ROTC studying Aerospace Engineering – stepping courageously down my path to becoming an astronaut. About this time, I decided to get my private pilot's license. A neighbor, who was also a pilot, offered to take me flying. Of course, I took him up on his offer – I couldn't wait to get up in the air!!

The first day he had available happened to be the day after my senior prom. Like most prom nights, ours was an all-night affair, ending with a very greasy sausage, egg and pancake breakfast at a friend's house. I got home and grabbed a quick nap. I woke up in time to wash my new car before my lesson (I was somewhat obsessive about the cleanliness of my car and washed it all the time). It was hot outside, but I was invincible! Then, off I went to the airport. I had no idea what to expect, but I was so excited! Up we went, but as the flight went on and on, I started feeling worse and worse. During the final few minutes of the flight, my greasy breakfast came back to haunt me, and I spent the rest of the flight with my head in a bag.

I was embarrassed and humiliated, but I never thought about quitting even once. The next summer I started flying lessons. I took a job on a grounds maintenance crew at a country club to pay for my lessons. I was also on a women's softball team that competed at the semi-pro level. Whenever I wasn't at work or playing softball, I was at the airport doing whatever I could do to push myself closer to completing the requirements for my license. I progressed from first lesson to my pilot's license in less than three months. It was an incredible push, and it shouldn't have been possible (most people take at least a year to earn their pilot's license), but I made the decision and had the discipline to do whatever it took to make it happen in one summer.

Accountability

Accountability is so important to individual and business success that I have devoted an entire chapter to it later in the book. In a nutshell, accountability is the concept of being answerable or responsible to someone for some particular action. You can be the most disciplined person in the world, but if there is no accountability, it is easy to wander off course. It is the rare individual indeed who can successfully hold himself accountable day in and day out. Most people need some manner of outside accountability for it to be meaningful and motivating. When you are accountable to another person and you have to share your progress with that person regularly, something shifts inside – it lights a fire under you. The idea of not performing or of letting the person you are accountable to down becomes intolerable.

Many companies use some form of accountability, but often they are using it in the wrong way – rather than using it as a means of motivating people to higher levels of achievement than they ever thought possible, they use accountability as a stick to force people to do certain things. Force negates everything. Accountability is an incredibly powerful tool; used properly it lights a creative fire that will burn out of control and propel you forward at lightning speed. More on that in Chapter 6.

> *I honestly have hundreds of examples where I have used the accountability concept to either get things done myself or to get others to rise to higher levels of achievement. One memorable example was when I joined the Corps of Cadets at Virginia Tech; I essentially signed a very powerful accountability agreement on that day. One of the provisions of being in the Corps was that if you quit you had to leave the university as well (except at certain times during the year). There were logistical reasons for this, but the fact is that freshman year for a new cadet is pretty tough, and, if it were easy to quit, the Corps would lose too many people every year. So, as a new cadet I was held accountable by the university itself to persist through the semester; if I quit, I was putting my entire college career on hold until the next semester. That's a big deal!! I did not necessarily enjoy my new cadet year all the time - it was difficult*

and even scary sometimes, but I never even considered quitting because I would be letting down myself, my parents, my fellow cadets, the Corps itself – everyone to whom I considered myself accountable. The "pain" associated with quitting (dropping out of college) far exceeded anything I had to endure during that first year.

Standards

Setting high standards is absolutely essential to success – be it in your personal life, on your team, in your organization or in your business. It amazes me what some businesses will accept in terms of performance from their employees – the salesperson who makes two sales calls per month because all he does is paperwork, the sales manager who will promise anything to get a sale even if he knows he can't deliver on his promises, the secretary who is on personal phone calls or instant messaging on Facebook all day, the production worker who spends more time in the break room than on the production line, the cashier who grumbles and complains to every customer, the rude customer service associate who treats every client as a burden. It's not enough to have a warm body occupying a chair! If an employee is not adding value to your organization, you are flushing money down a toilet every single day that they are on the payroll. Worse yet, it is not at all uncommon for these substandard employees to drag down the morale and the productivity of the entire organization.

Without standards for performance, how do you sort the "eagles" from the "turkeys?" You can't be sure who is sub-standard if you haven't actually set the standards to begin with. The military is genius when it comes to standards – if you don't cut the mustard you are done! In any organization you are only as strong as the people who are working for you; you have to be willing and able to weed out the bad and recognize the good. You are never going to get where you want to go by looking the other way.

Likewise, in your personal life you will only achieve as high as you reach. If you set high standards for yourself, you will achieve at a high level. If you are content to just get by, well then, don't expect much out of life.

> *When I was an Instructor Pilot, as I mentioned earlier, I was responsible for passing or failing the students I instructed. It was not easy to fail a student, but I took my responsibility incredibly seriously because I was dealing, quite literally, with people's lives. Beyond that was my responsibility to the Air Force to ensure that only students who met their strict, exacting standards were allowed to move on to become pilots. A warm body in a seat wasn't going to do it. Each of the students I flew with had to meet incredibly high standards to move to the next stage of their training. Because of the high standards set by the Air Force and the high standards that I held myself to, I knew exactly what I needed to do to perform my job as effectively as possible. Standards enabled*

me to put feelings aside and do what needed to be done for the good of all. Those standards ensured that the Air Force had mission ready pilots who were prepared to handle whatever eventuality might occur in their aircraft.

Systems

Systems are amazing tools for your business and your life. Essentially, they are "scripts" for how certain things need to be done. The military makes great use of systems – pretty much everything anyone does in any branch of the military has a protocol associated with it. Successful companies are the same way; there are policies and procedures that detail how certain things are to be executed.

When I started my business, I drew upon my military experience and took the advice of a mentor who suggested that I run my business from Day #1 as if I already had thousands of clients. This was incredibly powerful business advice, and I am so grateful that I listened to it because the systems I put in place early on and have continued to develop over the years have allowed the company to grow efficiently and effectively.

Of course, this is where discipline, accountability and standards come into play. Systems are only effective when they are implemented and followed! If your employees don't follow the systems then you have a bunch of people doing their own thing with little or no consistency – that leads to shoddy product, poor customer service, and ultimately big trouble for your business ororganization.

Systems can have a profound effect on your personal life as well. I use systems and tools all the time in my everyday life and I urge you to do the same. Many of the tools I use everyday are laid out in the pages of this book – they work for business and they work personally –imagineering, daily commitment sheets, accountability agreements, just to name a few. My personal systems give me a daily roadmap to follow so I stay on the path to my goals and avoid getting sidetracked.

> The Air Force relies on systems in every facet of their operations, and you can imagine how strict those systems are when it comes to the handling of nuclear weapons. For instance, mission ready aircraft with nuclear armaments are parked in a designated area that is marked off by a thick red lined perimeter. No one without specific clearance is allowed within that perimeter and the aircraft are guarded by military police with very large guns and orders to "shoot first, ask questions later." Shortly after I separated from the Air Force, I was working as a civilian flight instructor on Maxwell Air Force Base in Montgomery, Alabama. Now, there were no aircraft permanently assigned to Maxwell AFB; it did not have any aircraft of its own. It was a headquarters base, and its mission centered around training; however, its flight line was always busy with visiting dignitaries, transient aircraft and the like.

REMARKABLE COURAGE

One day I was working with a student who was ready to fly solo for the first time, so I got out of the plane and started making my way to the air control tower while he readied for takeoff. On this particular day, a nuclear armed F-16 fighter had stopped at Maxwell to refuel, so all of the required protocols were in place: The area around the jet was isolated by a red line on the tarmac around its perimeter, armed guards were on duty, etc. Unfortunately, I was unaware of the visitor. I was walking to the tower, concentrating on my student and his upcoming flight and was not paying much attention to what was going on around me. All of a sudden I heard "FREEZE! Don't move! Get your hands up!" I looked up and saw men with machine guns running at me from all directions. Then I looked down and saw that my foot was just inside a red line on the ground.

It only took an instant for the full gravity of the situation to hit me. I had activated "the system" and nothing was going to stop the ensuing chain of events. I was handcuffed, placed under arrest and told I was being charged with the attempted theft of a nuclear weapon. I was put in a squad car and taken to police headquarters for processing. Now, it became clear very quickly to everyone involved that neither the jet nor its weaponry were in any way threatened, but there

> was a system to be followed, protocols to be executed, and heads would roll if they weren't. Everyone involved, including me, followed the system and the situation was resolved quickly. I was at the police station for about 15 minutes and then they let me go and drove me back to the flight line where I met my student who was just finishing up his flight, none the wiser. No charges were filed and life returned to normal, except that I have one heck of a funny story to tell.

In some ways the whole chain of events may seem rather ridiculous, but stop and think for a moment: Can you imagine what would happen on a base where there were dozens of nuclear armed jets and there were no systems in place? Or the catastrophic consequences that could ensue if each individual airman was allowed to use his judgment in determining who was and was not a threat? The system ensures that a procedure is followed and that there is no room for subjective judgment in a situation that could threaten your life or the life of your business.

Discipline, accountability, standards, and systems are an incredibly powerful recipe for success. It's all about strategy. It's all about tools. It's all about integrating these four pillars of success into the foundation of everything you do. Unfortunately, you see, it's not enough to just KNOW this information. There is a whole science behind implementation. Everyone knows things they need to be doing to achieve the results they want in their business or in their personal life, but they don't do them. Worse yet, people know that doing certain things will give them the exact opposite of the result they desire, and yet they do them anyway.

It is one thing to possess information, but changing behavior so that you – and your employees or team members – actually implement that knowledge is something else entirely. Once you understand and internalize the process of bridging this "information-action gap," you can go on to create whatever results you want – and that's where the real magic occurs.

2 | AIM HIGH

Before you can embark on the journey to success, you have to know two things – where you are and where you want to go. So many people and companies go for years without really taking stock of where they are and what they are moving towards. Teams practice the same way for years, hoping that this year will be different and they will finally win the championship. They keep doing the same things, day after day, year after year, and wonder why they stay stuck – why things don't get better.

As far as we can prove, you only get one life – ONE! Shouldn't each and every day be filled with joy and abundance? Shouldn't you savor your life experiences and relish the growth from them, rather than just endure them, taking one step closer to the grave with each passing day?

A Goal GPS

Sadly, most people just accept what they are given in life, rather than going out and deliberately CREATING what they really want out of life. So many people just let life happen to them and then end up wondering where their lives went and what it was all for – all because they are scared. I say forget that!! When I set a goal for myself or for my business, if it doesn't scare the hell out of me then it's just not big enough! I am positively *unreasonable* when it comes to setting the bar for my own achievement – I will not settle for less than incredibly, overwhelmingly amazing!

So I ask you... Where are you and where do you want to go? Not where do you think you can get; not what do you think you should settle for. WHAT DO YOU WANT?? What do you REALLY want? To answer this question you have to suspend logic – there is no weighing the pros and the cons here. You won't have any clue HOW you are going to achieve your goal (and if you do know how, then it's not the right goal – it's just sideways movement and there is no growth in that). Finding the right goal is like falling in love - you will know it in your gut when it is the right one! When I set a goal, if I don't start giggling over the absurdity and audaciousness of it – if the hairs on my arms don't stand on end at the thought of it, it's not the right one.

Where are you and where do you want to go? Think about going on vacation. When you decide to take a vacation, you sit down and make some decisions and some plans. Where do you want to go? How do you want to travel (direct, fastest route in a jet; or take your time and drive and see the countryside along the way)? What do you need to take with you? And on it goes. Without a clear destination, you'll never get there. Imagine loading your packed suitcases and your family or friends in the car, turning the key and getting to the end of the driveway. Now what? Without a predetermined destination, which way do you turn?

Do you want to be a billionaire? Great! Do you want to have the most amazing relationship with your perfect soul mate? Wonderful! Do you want to double your income or quadruple the revenue of your department or company? Perfect! Do you want to win the world championship in your sport? Awesome! This is the star at which you are aiming – it's the ultimate destination.

So, where do you want to go? What's your destination? It may be extremely difficult to decide, especially if you are one of those people who has spent a good deal of time "sleepwalking" through life, but you *must* decide. You must have the courage to dare to dream.

Do some serious soul searching, suspend logic, use your imagination. Choose your destination. Now, the next question is: Where are you right now? I'll go back to the analogy of taking a trip. If you know you want to go to California, but you have no idea where you are currently, how do you know which way to turn? So, take stock of your current situation. If your goal is to be a billionaire and you currently have $10 in the bank with ten days to go before pay day – that's okay, that's where you are starting from. If you want the ideal relationship with your soul mate and you are currently stuck in an abusive relationship with a cruel partner who makes you feel like garbage most days, that's fine – that is your starting point. If you want to quadruple the revenue of your company, but you just had to lay off 30% of your workforce or you want to win the world championship but you came in last place last year – so what, that's YOUR starting point.

When you look at where you are in relation to this huge gigantic goal that you have set for yourself, it can be really humbling and disheartening – it may seem utterly impossible for you to reach your destination. But I will tell you this: no matter what your current condition may be and no matter how gigantic and unreasonable your ultimate goal may be, if you have a burning desire to achieve it, the expectation that you will achieve it, the belief that you can achieve it and you take action toward it each day – there is NOTHING you cannot do!!

We Think In Pictures

Once you have determined your goal and taken stock of where you are currently in relation to that goal, the next step is to paint a picture of what your destination looks like? And even more importantly, you need to determine what it FEELS like? As you'll soon discover, the actions you take in life don't occur based on what you know; they are based upon what you FEEL. So when you are in pursuit of a goal, it's crucial that you understand what it will feel like to have what you are going after. You have to KNOW that you know that you know that the goal you are going after is already yours.

Why? Well, it comes down to the way we, as human beings, think. When I am working with a client, I start by making the distinction between the mind and the brain, but a simple discussion is never enough; I have to add a visual image of what the mind "looks" like. See, when you and I think, we literally think in pictures. And the clearer the picture you have of something, the more order and the less fear, doubt, and confusion you experience. Think about it: if I ask you to think of your car, a picture or an image of your car will flash on the screen of your mind; not your mom's car, or your friend's car or the letters C-A-R., but your car. And the thing is, this is working all the time, whether you want it to or not. As human beings we think in pictures – PERIOD.

Don't believe me? Well, let me prove it to you. Right now, no matter what you do, DON'T.............. think about a pink elephant. What just happened? Did you see a picture of a massive pink thing with big ears and a long nose flash across your mind? I'm willing to bet so. It is a basic fact: as human beings, we think in pictures.

So, in order to begin the process of moving toward your destination – your goal – you have to develop a picture in your mind of where you want to go.

> *As I was approaching the end of high school, my dream was to be an astronaut – I absolutely loved everything about the space program, and with all my heart and soul I wanted to pilot the space shuttle. I spent so much of my time dreaming about blasting off from Cape Canaveral and looking back at Earth from space. I had a very clear picture of what my life as an astronaut would look like, and I was very emotionally involved with that vision. I not only SAW it, I FELT it!! It gave me direction. A huge dream like that doesn't just happen, and I wasn't content to simply dream about it. I knew I had to take action to make it happen. So I worked my tail off on the grounds crew at the local Country Club to earn the money it took to hire an instructor to teach me how to fly. I was 19 years old and in 3 short months I earned*

my private pilot's license. I decided to attend college at Virginia Tech and enroll in the Corps of Cadets and Air Force ROTC which put me on a path to graduate with a commission as an officer in the United States Air Force. I decided to major in Aerospace and Ocean Engineering so I could spend four years essentially pairing my two great loves – airplanes and math. All along I had a picture in my mind of where I was going and every single day I took action to take a baby step toward my dream. Without such a clear vision of my destination, I would likely have wandered aimlessly through college – like so many of my friends – changing majors, focusing on fun rather than academics, perhaps dropping out all together. My vision gave me the courage to persist each and every day, come what may, despite overwhelming odds and obstacles every step of the way.

The Dream Machine

So, how do you define your dream? Dreams are funny things. Ask any child what s/he wants to be when s/he grows up and you will get all sorts of "illogical" answers. I asked that question of my 9-year old son, Josh, and the answer was "I'm going to be the quarterback for the New England Patriots, a professional bowler, a storm chaser and a trash guy" – and he meant it too! Kids don't know about logic and limitations, so they believe anything is possible. And guess what? THEY ARE RIGHT!!! Anything IS possible; however, the older you get the more chained to your circumstances you become. Logic and safety are the order of the day, and it gets harder and harder to crank up those "dream machines" that worked so well when you were a child. It gets harder and harder to build those big, beautiful, vivid pictures of what you want to be, do or have in your life. You get used to justifying the status quo – to the point of berating yourself if you start dreaming too big. You tell yourself that you should be happy with what you have – after all, you ARE so much better off than so many people you know.

That's how you go through life until the day you die, stuck in a rut of self-imposed limitations and circumstances. That's why businesses stall, get stuck in a rut, decline and eventually close their doors. Does any of this resonate with you? Well, I'm going to help you get unstuck – I'm going to give you the tools you need – chapter by chapter – to break the bonds of logic that are holding you in place so you can create the life that you want.

So let's get to it. The first thing you need to do is develop a clear picture of your destination – your goal – so your mind can work with it. The following questions will help you crank up those rusty "dream machines." Remember, we think in pictures – it is the ONLY way we think, so the only way your mind can take your desire and move it into reality is if it has a picture to work with.

Now, here's where it gets tricky. See, logic is probably yammering away in your ear right now, telling you this is a bunch of silly, new age, woo-woo nonsense. I assure you that I have absolutely no time in my day for whimsical, frou-frou wishful thinking; however, I'll be brutally honest with you right now... If you keep doing what you've always done, you're going to keep getting what you've always gotten. This is one of those times when you need to find the courage to push logic aside, think outside the box and step outside your corporate image or team culture and try something new – something that works if you believe it will.

The following 9 questions are designed to get your dreamers turned on and worked out a little bit. Spend some focused time with them and be specific and detailed when answering them. If you want to be financially prosperous, don't just write "I want more money." With such a general statement, if you go out into the parking lot and find a penny on the ground – BAM! – the universe has done its part and you're done. You have "more" money. Instead, how much money do you want? What would you do with the money once you have it? What kinds of things are you doing then that you can't do now? How do you feel about yourself? How do other people treat you? Are you a role model for others? How do your social interactions change? Imagine you are holding Aladdin's lamp in your hands and you are granted unlimited wishes and that you are guaranteed to be completely successful. What do you dare to dream if you are guaranteed success? Get so detailed and specific that if someone else read what you wrote, they would see the same picture in their mind that you see in yours – the more detailed, the better!

1. What is your goal? What, specifically, do you want to be, to do or to have?
2. Why do you want it?
3. In what ways will your life/business/organization/team be different when you have reached your goal?
4. What one thing are you looking forward to most when you reach your goal?

5. What have you always wanted to do, but were afraid to try?

6. Assume for a moment that money is no object. What does your perfect wardrobe look like? What kind of car would you drive? What kind of house would you live in? What does your dream office look like? What charities would you contribute to? How much would you give?

7. Who do you want to be – how do you want to see yourself?

8. What are your talents and how are you using them? How do you WANT to use them?

9. What would make you jump out of bed every morning, excited about the day ahead?

Now that you have blown the cobwebs from your "dream machine", use the feelings that you have generated to write a detailed description of as many facets of your life/organization as you can think of once you have achieved your goal.

I call this process "imagineering" and I'll go into it in great detail in Chapter 5 because it is something that you really want to incorporate into your daily life – just like taking a shower or brushing your teeth. Walt Disney was the master of this technique. He used it to turn a swamp into the vacation mecca of the world in Orlando, Florida.

Here are the rules, the STANDARDS for imagineering:

- **Start your vision statement with** *"I am so happy and grateful now that I ..."* **Your description should be in the present tense, as if you are living that life right now.**
- **Be vivid and detailed in your narrative to the point that a stranger could read it and have the same image in their mind that you see in yours. The more detailed you are, the clearer the image in your mind, the quicker you will see results!**
- **Give absolutely NO energy to what you don't want – only consider what you DO want.**

Remember that this is a dream, a fantasy – make sure you are writing what you really WANT, not what you think you can get – not what you think you SHOULD be happy with – it's all about what you WANT!!! Put your logic aside and have fun! I know you've been taught just the opposite in the business world, but do it anyway!

Tool: The Goal Card

The goal card is a powerful tool that acts as a trigger to keep your ultimate goal in your conscious awareness throughout the day. As life gets busy, it can be easy to "take your eye off the ball" with regard to what you are really working toward. The goal card is simply a small card (like a business card or small index card) that you write your goal on and then carry with you in your pocket or purse. On it you write "I am so happy and grateful now that…" and then write something that you REALLY want. You don't have to have any clue how you are going to get it; you just have to WANT it.

Take it out and read it as often as possible (reading it aloud to yourself is even better). It is the repetition of the ideas that changes your thinking by allowing you to take your mind off of your present circumstances and focusing it on what you want. For example: "I am so happy and grateful now that revenue has exceeded $5,000,000 per year and we have more than 1,000 clients." Another example could be: "I am so happy and grateful now I have $1,000,000 of disposable income in my bank account to spend freely on myself and others." Yet another example might be: "I am so happy and grateful now that I am married to my soul mate and live a life of indescribable joy and happiness. We are each other's reason for being and are so incredibly happy together."

Goal cards work in any area of your life!! (You can download a complimentary goal card from my website at DebCheslow.com).

3 | BASIC TRAINING

Anyone who knows me knows that I am a huge advocate of weight lifting, but it's not your physical muscles that I am talking about in this case – it's your mental muscles! I have never met a man or woman, including myself, that couldn't use some serious mental calisthenics in their life! Your mind is the key; by harnessing the incredible power of your mind, you will be successful in any venture you set out to master.

Your Magnificent Mind

The mind holds the key to unlocking the unlimited potential within each one of us, yet the vast majority of people fail to ever really tap into this powerful force. Why is that? Well, one big problem is that far too many people have no idea what "MIND" is. MOST people use the terms "mind" and "brain" interchangeably, but this misconception could not be farther from reality – they are, in fact, very different and distinct. I like to describe the brain as the radio and the mind as the music. The music is transmitted through the radio; it doesn't originate from it. Much in the same manner the brain is the biological organ inside the skull and your thoughts don't originate from it. The brain is on the physical plane – you can see it, measure it, study it, etc. Mind, however, is movement – it's on the spiritual plane.

Mind is an activity found in every cell of our being. Think about it for a minute: it is rumored that Albert Einstein's brain is housed in a jar in a laboratory somewhere in New Jersey, but it's of absolutely no use to anyone (other than those who may have studied it's anatomy and structure) because Einstein's MIND isn't with it any longer. The brain is a physical organ, and its functions include muscle control and coordination, sensory reception and integration, and speech – it's an electrical and chemical switching station. The brain is a part of our central nervous system while the mind controls the higher functions, such as memory, reason and thought. The mind is the description of our conceptualization of what we think, analyze and project.

The mind, has two separate and distinct facets: the **Conscious** mind and the **Subconscious** mind.

As we already established in Chapter 2, human beings think in pictures – it is the only way we can process thoughts. Because the mind is not on the physical plane, no one has ever seen it – and no one ever will - there is no picture. Yet, as human beings, we think in pictures so for us to have a true understanding of the mind, we have to be able to generate a clear mental picture to work with. No picture leads to confusion. So, we need a picture of the mind to work with.

In 1934, Dr. Thurman Fleet, a chiropractor and founder of the Concept Therapy Institute, was working with his patients to literally heal themselves of ailments by "thinking" themselves healthy; however, he kept running up against this same roadblock when discussing the mind's role in healing the body. They had no visual frame of reference for the concept of "mind." Dr. Fleet decided that since our thoughts are visual, we must have a picture of the mind in order to harness its power.

As a result of his decision, a very simple yet profound tool known as the "Stick Person" emerged. Dr. Fleet's drawing brings order and understanding to our mind and is a fantastic tool we can use to explain how our thoughts affect how we see ourselves and ultimately determine our results. It makes absolutely no difference that Dr. Fleet actually made up the picture – as long as we can associate an image with a concept, we can develop understanding and application. So, now, let's examine the following image of the Stick Person.

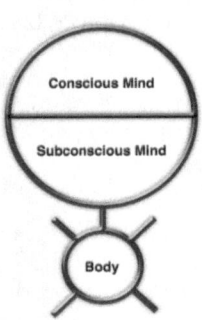

It's kind of funny, isn't it? We start with a version of the stick figure person that every one of us drew a million times in kindergarten, only in this version the head is purposely drawn disproportionately larger than the body. This is because the mind is the dominant force in our lives, not the body; the body is merely an instrument of the mind; that is, the body carries out the "commands" it receives from the mind. Then, we add a horizontal line bisecting the head into two halves. The top half of the head is the Conscious Mind, or our thinking mind, and the lower half is the Subconscious Mind, or our emotional mind.

Thoughts (in our conscious mind) cause us to experience feelings (in our subconscious mind), which drive the body into action, which in turn lead us to manifest the results we are getting in our lives. What I want you to start understanding is that our results are ultimately driven by our thoughts, but not by thoughts *alone*. Feelings will always come into play. If you can change your thoughts to produce different *feelings* to drive your body into different actions, you cannot fail to achieve different results.

In order for you to replace your old, outdated thoughts that are keeping you stuck in place with new thoughts that will move you in the direction of your goals, you must have a clear and concise comprehension of how your mind works. Don't get nervous here; I'm not talking psychiatry or psychology – I'm an Aerospace Engineer, for heaven's sake - this is not complicated stuff. The only thing is that we've never been taught this information before, but with a very elementary understanding of how your mind functions, you have the ability to tap into an immense power that lies largely dormant within yourself. Let's take the Stick Person apart piece by piece and see what's really going on here.

THE CONSCIOUS MIND

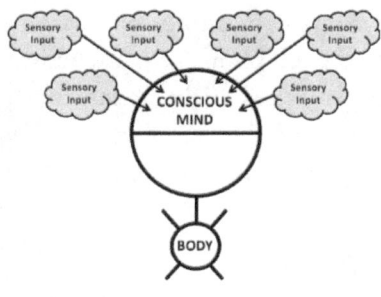

Your Conscious Mind is your thinking mind. This is where your free will resides. The conscious mind has the ability to accept or reject any idea introduced to it. Your five senses—sight, hearing, taste, touch, and smell are continually pumping in sensory inputs and stimuli from your outside environment. The conscious mind reads and interprets the inputs received from your physical senses. Because you think in pictures, anytime one or all of your five senses is triggered you immediately create a picture in your mind. This is much like a satellite dish that transmits signals to your television set or a cell phone tower that transmits signals to your smartphone.

Think of your conscious mind as the highway that all this external information travels on to enter your subconscious mind. Various feelings are generated depending on the different interpretations you give to these external stimuli. For instance, does the smell of a certain perfume bring back memories of your grandmother? Or does the taste of a cherry snow cone remind you of the beach or summer afternoons spent at the swimming pool as a child? As these sensory inputs are received, your conscious mind has the power to accept or reject the thoughts associated with them. If the conscious mind chooses to accept the thoughts, the subconscious mind has no choice but to generate the feelings triggered by those thoughts.

Everything on the physical plane is a manifestation of thought. Everything in your awareness—everything you see that is manmade—it all started as a thought. The clothes you are wearing, the ATM machine you grabbed $20 from this morning, the chair you are sitting on, the house you live in, the cell phone your friend just texted you on - EVERYTHING began as a thought, as someone's unrealistic fantasy. You have to understand that all of your bodily experiences are an expression of your mind, your thoughts.

The Subconscious Mind

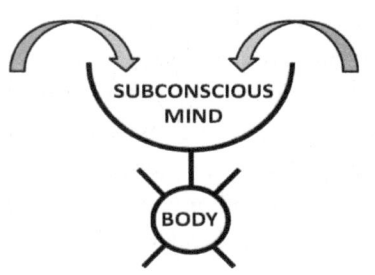

As I mentioned before, the subconscious mind has no ability to reject any idea or thought impressed upon it; it simply must accept every suggestion made to it—it is your emotional or feeling mind. By assembling various facts, your conscious mind draws conclusions which generate emotions and feelings in your subconscious mind.

For example, if you go into work and your boss calls you into his office and tells you that you have done such a great job that he is promoting you and giving you a much better office and a 25% salary increase, your conscious mind processes those sensory inputs and impresses the information on your subconscious mind. You can't help the FEELINGS that well up inside you – happiness that all your hard work and long hours have been recognized, pride in your accomplishment, excitement that you can finally take your lover on that cruise s/he wants to go on, etc. Likewise, if instead your boss tells you that you're fired, you can't help the feelings that are generated – disappointment, failure, self-deprecation, embarrassment, etc. The thoughts in your conscious mind cause feelings/emotional responses in your subconscious mind. Each thought you think and accept is impressed upon the subconscious part of your mind, and it can't tell the difference between what is real and what is imagined; it accepts everything as fact.

THE BODY

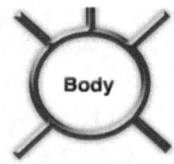

The body is the smallest part of the Stick Person. It is drawn this way to illustrate the concept that your physical body is merely an instrument of your mind and is your outward physical manifestation to the world. Although it may not seem like it, your body is fairly insignificant and weak when compared with your mind; however, without the body there can be no action, and therefore, no results. Before you can CREATE what you want in your life you must DECIDE what you want and then you must take ACTION toward your goal EVERY DAY!! It would be so great if you could just close your eyes tight and clasp your hands and think "$1,000,000 - $1,000,000 - $1,000,000" and have a million dollars suddenly appear in your bank account, but, sadly, that's not how it works.

Let's get real here: Would you agree that you KNOW things you should be doing to get better results in your life? Sure you do. You hold the information in your conscious mind. I like to illustrate this point with the example of dieting because it is something that almost everyone can relate to. Does this scenario sound vaguely familiar? Monday morning you wake up and start your new diet. You eat according to the plan you've chosen to follow. You get up three days that week and head to the gym and exercise. You do everything you're supposed to do for that whole week, and, on the following Monday, you get on the scale and find that you have lost 4 pounds. You do the weight-loss happy dance around your bathroom and head off for another great week on your diet plan. But, this week, somewhere around Saturday, you're at the food store and you pass the bakery and that piece of 14 layer chocolate cake starts calling your name. Or, the alarm clock goes off and you hit the snooze button because you feel like sleeping in instead of going to the gym. Or, your best friend calls and wants you to meet him at the local sports bar to watch the game and have a beer. You KNOW you should not put the cake in your basket, that you should get up and hit the gym, that you should not have a beer at the bar, but you FEEL like doing it. You may resist for a time, but, eventually, you give in to your feelings. You can KNOW all day long, but in the end, if you FEEL like doing something, you will do it. We'll get into how we overcome this "Information-Action Gap" in the coming chapters. Again, it's so simple, just not necessarily easy.

Your Weapons Arsenal

All too often people look at those who have achieved great success in their lives and assume that they were born into wealthy families or that perhaps they received advanced education that taught them things that "regular people" just don't know or that they were just flat out lucky; however, when you actually study the historic figures who are held up as iconic examples of personal or professional success, you'll find that many of them had to overcome incredible odds to achieve their success. For example, Thomas Edison only had a third grade education. Henry Ford's road to success was littered with all kinds of potholes and obstacles. The Wright brothers were not born into great wealth – they were simple bicycle mechanics. What they did have at their disposal was an incredibly well developed set of mental muscles – or Intellectual Faculties - that they had developed to such a degree that they could create pretty much anything they wanted in their lives.

These conscious faculties give your mind its creative power – they separate you, as a human being, from a pig or a horse; however, I'm willing to bet that you have no clue what these faculties are, much less how to use them to create your dream life, and that's the problem – you are taught from your earliest moments to live from the outside in (Look at your brother, Listen to your teacher, Watch that kid...) rather than from the inside out. Instead of creating your reality, you simply accept what you are given in life. If I asked you to list your five senses, I'm sure you could do it without missing a beat – most five year olds can do that. On the other hand, if two people in 100 can tell me even three of their six intellectual faculties I would be amazed!

Sadly, the fact that you are unaware of the existence of your conscious faculties doesn't stop you from using them all the time – the problem is, you likely use them against yourself, rather than for yourself. It's the proper use of these intellectual faculties that will help you control the way you think. They're very much like mental muscles, and, just like physical muscles, they can be developed and made stronger through regular use and exercise. When used properly, you can create pretty much whatever it is that you want in your life.

The six Intellectual Facilities are:

1. **Will**
2. **Imagination**
3. **Perception**
4. **Reason**
5. **Intuition**
6. **Memory**

These faculties are always at work, but, like I said before, more often than not, people unconsciously use them against themselves. Let's take a look at these mental muscles individually.

WILL

Will is the intellectual faculty that gives your mind real power. It's through the use of the will that you are able to concentrate. It has nothing to do with force (force negates everything); it is more like brute determination. Will is the ability to focus intently. Often people who have a well-developed Will are called stubborn, but that's not the case. Stubbornness is the lack of desire to change while Will is a chosen thought repeated until the desired result is reached. It's the ability to hold your goal or your vision or your purpose on the screen of your conscious mind over time so that the vision can begin to seep down into your subconscious mind. Your ability to concentrate, your ability to stay focused on one thing to the exclusion of all outside distractions is a function of the development of your Will.

The Will is to the mind what a magnifying glass is to the sun. If you lie in the sun for a couple of hours, you'll get a nice golden brown tan from the sun's rays; however, if you harness those same rays through a magnifying glass, you'll blister your skin in about six seconds. It's the same energy; it's just focused. *That's* what you have the ability to do with your will: hold your goal on the screen of your mind with focused intensity.

IMAGINATION

Imagination is your ability to create. Children have the greatest imaginations because logic and reality don't exist in their minds. Let a three year old loose in the Tupperware cupboard and what does s/he creates: space ships, cars, drums, buildings, trucks – you name it. Everyone has a brilliant imagination – it's just that somewhere around elementary school we stop using it. The same child who was making space ships out of plastic ware only a few years earlier heads off to school and starts looking out the window thinking about the games he's going to play with his friends at recess and... WHAM!! The teacher's hand comes down on his desk and he's told to "stop daydreaming, pay attention, daydreaming is for babies – you're a big boy now!" Instead of imagining and creating, we're taught to analyze everything and to look at the pros and cons. As we mature, we're trained to believe that imagination is "kid's stuff". This line of thinking is so wrong; we need to incorporate imagination into every aspect of our lives.

It's the imagination of SOMEONE that is responsible for the creation of everything within your current grasp - your computer, your pen, your desk, your home or office, your chair, your clothes - EVERYTHING had to be created or invented by someone and the first spark of that creative process came from someone's imagination. You have a brilliant imagination - RIGHT NOW - so start using it!! Understand that everything counts. Everything is fair game, and there is nothing that you can imagine that can't come to fruition somehow. Build pictures in your mind of the success you desire - totally ignore what you may consider to be your present constraints or obstacles - let your imagination take flight and concentrate on building the image of exactly how you want to live.

Your Imagination is a powerful force that can work for you or against you. You can either imagine how you can accomplish a goal or how you can't. All of these six Intellectual Faculties are always turned on, but you're not always using them the right way. You see most people will imagine all the reasons why things can't be done. They'll imagine all the obstacles. They'll imagine all the doom and gloom, and envision the worst case scenario. Well, whatever you focus on becomes your reality. So if you spend all of your time focusing on obstacles and failure, that's exactly what you will get.

Think about Steve Jobs of Apple Computers and Bill Gates of Microsoft for a moment. There's no doubt that any student of success would hold these two men up as great success stories. What if they had thought up their ideas and then "what if'ed" themselves into giving up? What if they had focused on all the obstacles that were in their way or on the possibility of failure and had stopped pursuing their dreams? Fortunately, that didn't happen – each of these men pursued their dream with a burning desire that burned so hot that they only saw what they wanted the result to be – and that is what each of them eventually got, and so much more.

Perception

Hill, W. E. "My Wife and My Mother-in-Law." Puck 16, 11, Nov. 1915.

Perception is the lens through which you see the world. Everyone approaches everything they come across in their life - every problem, opportunity, idea, person, etc. - from their own point-of-view - their own perception. Just because my perception of a situation is different from yours doesn't mean that I'm right and you're wrong (or vice versa). For instance, look at the cartoon to the left - what do you see? Do you see an attractive young woman or an ugly old woman? They're both in the picture and seeing one doesn't mean the other is NOT there.

Think about how many times in your life you've come upon a situation and you've determined it to be unworkable - you just couldn't do it. Well, you couldn't do it from your particular point-of-view at the time, but then someone else came along with an entirely different point-of-view and tackled the situation with apparent ease. That's what perception is - it's your point-of-view. Perception is the way you see your world. For every good there is a bad, for every up there is a down, and for every hot there is a cold. With this knowledge, you can use your Perception to view something as an obstacle or an opportunity. Instead of always perceiving events to be negative and asking yourself, for instance, "What if I my new business fails?", change the conversation and reverse the question to "What if I my new business is wildly successful?"

It is natural for people to interpret the events that occur in their lives based on past events and outcomes. Nothing has meaning, or is good or bad, until you make it so in your conscious mind.

Consequently, each person will have a different Perception or interpretation of exactly the same event or object. Think about a trial. The prosecution and defense each have different witnesses because each person has a different Perception of what really happened.

When I first started karate in June, 2003, the thought of breaking a stack of bricks was very intimidating to me, and I really couldn't see how it would be possible. In April 2004, I broke my first board (a 12" x 12" x 1" piece of pine) and began to believe that breaking bricks was possible, but I still didn't know how I would be able to do it. As time went on, I grew more skilled and more confident, until finally in March 2006 I was ready to give it a try. I stacked up three bricks in my basement and, although I was scared to death of what might happen, I succeeded in breaking them. I had a huge bruise on my hand and it hurt for weeks, but I did it! In December of that same year, I successfully broke four at our Christmas party demo. Again I had a sore hand for days, but I was proud because I thought I had done it "right". I was convinced that five bricks would be my limit, or maybe six. Then something amazing happened. In September 2007, I broke a stack

of five bricks at a street demo, but it didn't hurt and there was no bruise. At some point during that year, I had taken my first step towards becoming a true martial artist. My perception of my abilities began to change. I had learned to summon my inner strength (like a parent that can lift a car off of their pinned child). I then progressed to six bricks in December 2007; seven in February 2008; and eight (a feat few men can accomplish) in September 2008. What I have realized is that when I first broke three and four bricks, I was using pure strength. Now, when I break successfully, I summon my inner strength, black-out, and "wake-up" to see a pile of pieces and there is no pain or injury. It's all a matter of perception. I no longer perceive the breaking of eight bricks to be an impossible feat. My perception changed based upon my experience.

What if you could take something right now which you perceive to be impossible and turn it into reality? Well, you absolutely can – people who make their dreams come true do it every single day! Never underestimate the role of Perception in your daily life. It has the power to alter your attitude and course of direction almost without your notice. That being said, I hope you can see how easy it is to use your perception against yourself in any growth-oriented situation – to see a HUGE opportunity as an obstacle. When you change the way you look at life, your life changes.

Reason

Reason is your ability to think and choose. It is actually your free will and what separates you from the animals. Pigs can see, hear, smell, taste and touch, but they can't reason. They can't imagine. They can't look at their circumstances and decide to change them. You won't see a pig look up from his muddy sty and peer over at the horses in the grassy pasture and turn to his friend and say, "You know what, I'm done with this mud – I think I'm going to go live like a horse." Reason is the higher side of your own nature. We are the only species that has the ability to think and choose.

All of the great leaders throughout history – the historians, theologians, industrialists, politicians, scientists – they've all disagreed on virtually everything, but they did agree on one thing: we become what we think about most of the time. Your reasoning faculty is one of your most powerful tools, and yet, most people don't use it; most people don't think! You're probably saying to yourself, "Well, everyone thinks, Deb!" But that's just not true - hardly anyone actually *thinks* - mental activity does not necessarily constitute thought. George Bernard Shaw was so right when he said that 2% of the population thinks, 3% THINK they think and the other 95% would rather die than think. Earl Nightingale said, "If most people said what they were thinking they would be speechless!" Just listen to the conversations that are going on around you. Would most people say what they are saying if they were actually thinking? Would people do what they are doing if they were thinking?

Your reasoning factor gives you the ability, in your conscious mind, to take a power that flows into your consciousness and literally *originate* a thought. As one thought builds upon another, ideas are formed. There *is* a huge caveat here that you must bear in mind though. When you base your decisions on Reason (and logic) alone, you will quickly reject anything that doesn't match your current understanding. This is why so many people get a fantastic idea that could absolutely change their life and then dismiss it as sheer folly shortly thereafter. That is why brilliant ideas are often shot down by upper management, leaving the employee who conceived of the idea feeling useless, unappreciated, "small," disgruntled – because it is beyond that which they know and understand – they cannot reasonably, logically lay out a plan to make it happen. This guarantees that you will continue to act on ideas that keep you marking time and reject any idea that would move your life or your business forward. Your reasoning faculty gives birth to all manner of amazing thoughts and ideas, but you must push logic aside and look to your other intellectual faculties to process and evaluate those ideas - ideas that can and will change your life!

INTUITION

If you take the time to develop it, your intuitive faculty is one of the greatest tools you will ever have, but you must DECIDE to develop it. Dr. Wayne Dyer describes intuition in the following manner: "If prayer is you talking to God, then intuition is God talking back." Intuition is the mental faculty that allows you to literally tune in to the vibrations around you. You transmit and receive vibrations all day long - thought is energy and when you're thinking, you're transmitting energy. Intuition seems magical, so much so that some people call it a 6th sense, a coincidence or a hunch.

Have there been times in your life when you have been able to tell what a person is thinking without them saying a word? Have you gone to meet a friend for lunch and you could tell that something was bothering them the moment you saw them walk through the door? Or have you suddenly had a nagging urge to pick up the phone and call someone for no particular reason only to have them say, "You know, I was JUST thinking about you!" This is your intuition picking up on the vibration - the thought energy - of that other person. Intuition is an incredibly powerful tool once it is developed. There are people in my life with whom my intuitive factor is exceptionally keen – I know what my partner, Angie, is thinking before she ever opens her mouth to speak – same with my daughters - and I continue working to develop my intuition each and every day.

> *In the business world, I was always a one-woman show, and I always thought that's how it had to be. I have always been a perfectionist with OCD tendencies and was very much of the opinion that if I wanted something done right, I needed to do it myself. Several years ago, after shifting the focus of my business to be in alignment with my talents of speaking, consulting and training, I found that I still wasn't jumping out of bed every morning, excited about the day ahead. Although I was very happy with my choice of direction, there was too much operational "clutter" in the way. I was bogged down by all of the day-to-day necessities of running the business. I never even considered hiring someone to take on these tasks because, logically speaking,*

as a start-up company with limited revenue, I couldn't afford to "hire" (in the traditional sense) someone competent enough to get the job done. It certainly seemed unworkable in any traditional scenario. That's where Angie came into the picture. She was my star client and had expressed a desire to help out with my business. I was sitting in a training seminar one day when intuition screamed in my ear so loudly that I almost fell out of my chair. I suddenly just "knew" what the solution was: I needed to ask Angie to be my business partner. She was thrilled with the opportunity. She bought 50% of my company and we joined forces as equal partners. I had defied logic, listened to my intuition, and in the process found an incredibly competent operations director, who was completely vested in the success of the company. Instead of having to pay her a salary, she paid me to purchase half of the company, giving the company needed seed money for future growth. What a beautiful, perfect solution!

Intuition is that "little voice in your head" that speaks to you, trying to guide you in a particular direction - toward your true purpose. If you are going to be truly successful in life, then you must develop your intuition and listen to it. Learn to relax and follow those hunches. Resist the temptation to reason your way back into your comfort zone.

Memory

Did you know that you have a perfect memory? Everyone does! There are just a lot of people walking around who incorrectly believe they have a bad memory. Anything you exercise, you strengthen. For example, if I put my right arm in a sling and leave it there, over time it will atrophy and be rendered useless; however, if I lift weights with that arm every day instead, over time the muscles will become very well developed and the arm will be very strong. Your memory is no different and there are so many exercises you can do to strengthen your memory muscles.

> I have always been an exceptionally good student, and I earned nearly perfect grades. I attribute this, in great part, to having the ability to memorize whole sections of textbooks before my exams. I can actually read a question on a test and mentally flip to the page in the textbook where the answer is and skim the page until I find the answer to the question. I did this repeatedly during my high school and college careers, into my Air Force training and in my numerous professional certification trainings (in my most recent example, I scored a near perfect score of 97.5% on the examination to become a Certified Fitness Professional); however, as "photographic" as my memory is, I have always had an incredibly difficult time remembering people's names. I managed to memorize a 750 page technical training manual in six weeks and ace an exam, but couldn't manage to remember

the names of the six people I had dinner with last night? It seems ridiculous and it is! What happened was that I convinced myself early in childhood that I had a semi-photographic memory, but I also convinced myself that I couldn't remember names. It became part of who I am. I created both the success and the shortcoming.

You DO have a perfect memory. You just have to decide to use it and use it correctly. The other problem is that, all too often, you use your memory against yourself; you use your memory to recall instances of failure. Those memories seem to linger so much longer and be so much more intense than memories of success because that's what you focus on. It's high time you started using that amazing memory of yours to help you create the future you want rather than to keep you stuck in a past that you don't want! Focus on all the good in your life. Recall all the successes you've had in your life; remember all the great things that you have accomplished and all the obstacles that you've overcome. Use your Memory to bolster your confidence and self-esteem as you try something new because at some point everything was new to you – and yet you learned.

Now, imagine the infinite possibilities for your life if you take the time to develop all six of these intellectual faculties and put them to use in ways that move you toward your goals and dreams instead of away from them. Imagine where your business could go if every employee learned to do the same. Get excited; you have the power to do just that; the power to create your future just as I and so many of my clients are continuing to do.

Tool: Affirmations

An affirmation is a goal stated as if it were already true. Thinking, saying, or writing affirmations is an easy way to bring positive change into your life. Affirmations are a way to change your attitude by taking control of your conscious thoughts. Your current beliefs and habits have come about because of thoughts you have repeated over and over again until they became a part of who you are at your core. Many of these thoughts are productive and move you forward in life, but many are self limiting and destructive in nature. The repetition of this negative self-talk wreaks havoc on your self-image. It is next to impossible to feel motivated when you are skeptical that you can ever achieve the desired results. Replacing negative self-talk with affirmations, can, over time, help you build your belief in yourself and what you are capable of achieving. As you adopt more positive attitudes and feel encouraged, you will find it easier to take the actions that you need to take in order to get the desired results.

The great thing about affirmations is that they can work in any area of your life, whether you want to create success in your financial or professional life, build stronger relationships, or get incredibly healthy - anything!

> *My favorite affirmation is "I am so happy and grateful now that I always have time for the people and things that are important to me." It seems that my schedule is packed every single day and that not a single day goes by when I don't get absolutely overwhelmed by the length of my "to-do" list. When the feelings of overwhelm come, I sit back, close my eyes,*

> take a deep breath and say my affirmation, take another deep breath, exhale and feel a sense of peace and calm come over me. In that calm, creative state intuition always speaks to me, and I am able to pick an item on my list and get to work. I have yet to pick the wrong thing or to have the world stop spinning on its axis because something did not get done on a particular day.

Take some time to develop several affirmations that relate to the goals you have set or that help you feel successful in the face of stress. Pick your favorite three affirmations and write them on an index card. Keep them with your goal card, then take out the list and read them aloud to yourself as many times a day as you can to keep yourself in the right mindset. Affirmations are a great tool to keep you moving forward toward your dreams.

Some Examples of Affirmations:

I am so happy and grateful now that...

- I powerfully attract more and more customers to my business!
- It is becoming easier and easier for me to realize my sales goals!
- Every day in every way I am getting better and better!
- I have everything it takes within me to achieve all of my goals and dreams!
- My customers recommend me to others and the number of customers is increasing daily!

- My business is self-sustaining and growing explosively!
- My income level is rising higher and higher!
- I am a success at everything I do!
- I am the master of my thoughts! I create my life!
- I surround myself with positive people who support and empower me to be more, do more and have more!
- I make appointments with ease, confident in the value of what I am offering and respectful of the decision the other person is going to make!
- I step out and do things I have never done in order to have things I have never had!
- Money comes to me in increasing quantities through multiple sources on a continuous basis!

4 | What's Holding You Back?

What if I told you that your success in achieving whatever goals you have set for yourself hinges on your **belief** - way down deep in your soul – that you can do, have or be "it" (whatever "it" is)? It is absolutely true!! There is a basic formula for success for any goal you are pursuing in life, be it money, business growth, the career or relationship of your dreams, a new house or a new car. That formula states that **success** is a function of **burning desire, belief, expectancy** and **action**. The stronger each of the variables is, the faster success will happen, but –and here's the kicker – if any one of those variables is absent (scores a 0 on a scale of 1-10), your chance for success is also zero.

I said before that your success or failure hinges on your belief that it is possible to achieve what you are going after, but aren't the other variables just as critical? Yes, of course they are, but believing that you can actually accomplish what you are striving for is –for the vast majority of people – the hardest variable in the equation to score high marks on. Let's take a weight loss program, for example. If you are heavy or really out of shape, it can be fairly easy to build up a burning desire to be thin and physically fit because you can imagine all the wonderful benefits that await you – you can paint a picture in your mind and generate the necessary desire. When you find a weight control program that really resonates with you and you understand why the plan asks you to do what it prescribes and you buy into its philosophy, it is easy to expect that the excess weight will come off your body if you follow the plan. It can even be fairly easy to overcome inertia and move into action when your desire and expectancy are high enough. Belief, on the other hand, is a tricky one – belief is the dominion of your subconscious mind, and true belief in a thing is all wrapped up in your self-image (which is the compilation of all the "stuff" that fills your subconscious mind). This is why traditional "diets" work for a while and then stop working (actually, the diet doesn't stop working, but you stop working the diet because you succumb to your habits and your conditioning); you stop believing.

You are, first and foremost, a spiritual being – nothing, absolutely nothing, is impossible for you. You MAKE things impossible by buying into all the junk that has been stuffed in your subconscious mind – without your permission, we might add (I'll get into that shortly). Once you strip away all the garbage that is holding you back, you will find that you can do ANYTHING you decide to do, and with that realization you can begin to build your belief that you can have, do or be anything you choose.

The Sweet Spot

Do you have a "bucket list?" You know, that list of things you want to do, be or have before you "kick the bucket." If you have never taken the time to create a bucket list, you need to do so – right now would be a great time!! When you look at that list it can be so tempting to focus on "the how." HOW is that ever going to happen? HOW can I make this a Fortune 500 company in this economy? HOW will I ever win the championship? HOW am I ever going to afford that car? HOW am I ever going to earn that income? HOW will I ever attract my soul mate? HOW could I possibly lose that much weight? And on and on it goes. Well, if you keep focusing on the "how," you're not likely to ever achieve a big goal. What you must focus on instead is how you FEEL in any given moment and try to always feel "better." "Better" is a GREAT word! Now I know that sounds silly, childish and illogical, but stick with me here.

When I first developed my bucket list back in 2009, there were things on it that I had absolutely no clue how I was going to get, but I just knew that I wanted them. On the other hand there were things that I knew I could easily get with little effort at all. It is important when you look at an item on your bucket list that you evaluate how you feel about it. First of all, do you have a strong desire for it? Second, do you *believe* you can have it with little or no doubt? If you answer "Yes" to both of those questions you are in "the sweet spot" and it is just a matter of time before you get it. You see, when you want something with a burning desire and you have no doubt that you can have it, you feel better when you think about it. You start getting excited and feel like Christmas is tomorrow and you KNOW there are presents under the tree – you KNOW it's coming. In fact, you feel as though you already have it.

That kind of feeling puts out a strong attractive force and will pull to you all the people, the resources, the circumstances – whatever you require - to attain your goal. It sounds all metaphysical and magical, but it is science in action!! Now, on the other hand, if you think about what you want and you feel worse, then doubt is beginning to creep in. Your belief is going down because you are focusing on HOW it's going to happen and you can't see the path.

Right now I have an item on my bucket list that I want really badly. It's huge, unrealistic, and illogical – I have a burning desire for it – an obsession with it, in fact –and I KNOW I can have it, although I have no earthly idea HOW. But the "how" doesn't matter; I have 100% belief that I WILL have it and every time I think about it – which is nearly all the time – I literally "buzz" with excitement and anticipation. I know that Christmas is coming and Santa is bringing presents and the feeling of excitement just feeds on itself, because I know this big HUGE thing that I want is in the sweet spot, so I KNOW it's just a matter of time before it is, in fact, mine.

DID YOU JUST CALL ME AN ELEPHANT?

The question is, what, specifically, is keeping you stuck and how did it get there in the first place? In all my of keynote presentations, I use a circus elephant as a way to introduce what is going on.

Have you ever been to the circus or to a fair and seen the elephants standing around by the tents? Have you ever noticed the tiny stake to which one of the elephant's legs is tied or chained. Often the stake is just barely pounded into the ground. The elephant weighs a good ton or more and is incredibly strong. Why does he just stand there? Why doesn't he just lift up his foot and pull the stake out of the ground and walk away to freedom?

Well, when the elephant was brought into captivity he was a baby, and the first thing the trainer did was to chain the baby elephant's leg to a stake that was most certainly stronger than the elephant. The baby elephant's instinct for freedom was strong and he kicked and tugged and pulled and fought and did everything he could to get away, but the chain was stronger than he was. This struggle went on and on, hour after hour, day after day until one day, about six months later, the baby elephant stopped struggling and gave up. He resigned himself to the fact that there was no hope; that it is what it is. This was his life and he should be happy because he had it so much better than those other elephants out there – at least he had food and shelter and someone to pet him every now and then. The baby elephant grew to adulthood and, even though he is now exponentially stronger than the chain and stake that hold him in place, it never even occurs to him to just lift his foot and give a little tug and walk away to freedom. He has literally been conditioned to have no hope, when all the while the only thing holding him back is a bunch of self-imposed limitations.

Sadly, the vast majority of people are just like the elephant. They begin their lives with all kinds of huge dreams of what they want out of life, but, as time goes by and they get older, the bright light of those dreams grows faint and dim and eventually goes out completely, replaced by logic and plans and a world where, if you can't see the path to what you want, it must be foolishness and folly. Well, I just don't buy that and you shouldn't either!

You know, I can get in my car in the dark and start driving. The headlights of my car illuminate only about 200 yards of the road in front of me and yet when I reach the end of that 200 yard distance, I can see another 200 yards farther. I can drive from Florida to California at night, 200 yards at a time. It's the same way with the path to your ultimate goal. You won't be able to see all the steps from the starting point, but you go as far as you can see, and then you'll be able to see how you can go further – you just have to summon the courage to start the journey!

When you were born you didn't have a conscious mind – your conscious faculties don't develop for several years. So, as a baby, your subconscious mind was wide open and took in everything it heard going on around you. For the first few years of life, babies are like little sponges soaking in every sensory input they receive from their parents, their grandparents, their brothers and sisters, their babysitters, the television and radio, etc., right into their subconscious mind. Think about how quickly you learned to speak your native language. It's because there were no conscious faculties to get in your way – you just learned it. It's the same with learning how to walk – you didn't know anything about "self-imposed limitations," so you kept trying until one day you were walking. Think about how HARD some of the things you learned to do as a small child are – how IMPOSSIBLE they are for many adults. Have you ever tried to become fluent in another language as an adult or had to learn to walk or talk all over again after some traumatic injury? Think about all you are capable of if you can just get out of your own way!!!

So, as a baby and a small child you were taking all this information from your external environment into your subconscious mind like a vacuum; it sucked in every word, thought or action it came into contact with, and stored it all as truth. Your subconscious mind is a storage unit for all that has happened in your life. It stores your beliefs which include your emotional connections to the past. Think of it as a scrapbook containing all of your past experiences. What you feel, think or do forms the basis of your experiences, which are stored in the form of underlying impressions in the subconscious mind. This is why it is so difficult to release old, self-destructive thoughts or defeating behaviors. So think about it: What was going on around you when you were a child? What kind of information was your subconscious mind sucking in about the "truth" of life?

Take an honest look at your life. If you are struggling in some area or another and have been for as long as you can remember, think back to what was going on in your family when you were a child. If you are constantly struggling to make ends meet, did your parents have financial struggles? Did they argue about money? Whatever was happening in the environment you lived in during your earliest years was dumped into your subconscious mind and stored as truth – your beliefs.

In most cases, the people who "programmed" you when you were a child thought they were doing the very best for you. They loved you and wanted you to be the most fabulous version of you possible, but they were unaware of what was happening. Any image or pattern of images that is repeatedly impressed upon your subconscious mind becomes part of your habitual patterns. Once your conscious faculties develop, it takes repetition to form habits and beliefs, but as a baby with a wide open subconscious mind, it takes very little repetition for environmental stimuli to be stored as absolute fact.

Let's look at some examples. Did you know that most people who grow up in families that are dependent on the welfare system end up on the welfare rolls themselves as adults? Do you think that children who grow up in a family where their parent(s) can barely scrape by each month actually look forward to the day when they can drop out of school and go on welfare just like Mom and Dad? Of course not!! Those kids – like all kids – have great big, illogical dreams for their future. They have the courage to actually step into action and try to make those dreams a reality, but somewhere along the way, things don't quite go the way they planned and their conditioning takes over. Bit by bit they give up on their dream and at the end of the day, they find themselves on welfare too.

The same can be said about lottery winners. Everyone seems to think that winning the lottery – "hitting the jackpot" – will end all their worries and woes. The statistics, however, do not bear this out. The vast majority of people (80%) who win a lottery jackpot of $1,000,000 or more, file for bankruptcy within five years of collecting their prize. How can this be you ask? Well, if a person with a poverty consciousness (conditioning) has a large influx of money, their conditioning will have them act in ways that will get rid of that extra money as fast as possible because being "rich" is not who they are at their core.

Habits and Paradigms

A habit is something you do without conscious thought – like brushing your teeth (do you actually focus on each stroke of the toothbrush, when to swish, when to swallow, etc., or do you think about what you need to do once you get to the office or about what you'll have for dinner) or driving a car (can you imagine what would happen if you had to consciously think about all the steps you need to take to stop a car as you approach a stop light – I taught 2 teenagers how to drive; it is not pretty).

A collection of habits is known as a paradigm, and there are as many different paradigms as there are people – no two are exactly alike, because the experiences of no two people are exactly alike. It is that collection of paradigms that determines your self-image – what you believe you are capable of, what you believe you deserve in life, whether you will reach your goal or not.

Repeated Image ➡ *Habit* ➡ *Paradigm*
(Collection of Habits) ➡ *Self-Image*

See, your paradigms are stored in your subconscious mind and are expressed through your actions. So if your parents treated you like you were stupid, stubborn, lazy or fat, you came to believe it. Furthermore, your subconscious mind went into overdrive, making you act in ways that would ensure that you made that belief your reality. If your parents believed that "money is the root of all evil," then I'm willing to bet that you have some money issues in your life. Paradigms are the governing belief systems that determine your success in life, and the thing about paradigms is this: they're not even YOURS! Remember the baby with the wide open subconscious mind? Who "programmed" that baby's subconscious? His or her parents, right? Well, who programmed the parents? Yep, *their* parents and so on and so on. Some paradigms are GENERATIONS old. You know, I think if you're going to have a paradigm that's screwing up your life, then it's only fair that you should have some say in the matter!

I love the story of the daughter who cut the ends off the roast before placing it in the pan. Every Sunday night, she has her mother and father over for a roast beef dinner and before she puts the roast in the pan, she whacks off the ends. One Sunday, her parents arrived early, so her mother helped her in the kitchen. As soon as she saw her daughter cut off the ends of the roast, she asked, "Why do you do that?" Her daughter replied, "Because you always did." Her mother looked at her and contemplated why they both threw away two perfectly good pieces of meat each time they baked a roast. She quickly realized that she saw her mother do the same and then decided to call and ask why. When the mother and daughter asked Grandma why she cut the ends off of the roast before putting it in the pan, they were astonished at the answer. There was no secret recipe or special reason; the Grandmother simply didn't have a pan big enough to cook a roast in. The only thing handed down from generation to generation in this story was an erroneous belief.

So what are YOUR paradigms? Well, if you want to know what you have been thinking subconsciously, just take a look at your present results. Are you overweight? Are you constantly struggling to make ends meet? Do your personal relationships leave something to be desired? Do you have difficulty keeping a job? Does your team keep losing? Is your business struggling? Keep in mind, paradigms surrounding money are some of the most common paradigms passed down through the generations.

Watch Out For The Crabs

There is a fantastic essay by Susan Raines-Bridges called "The Miracle of the Crab Pot" that really speaks to the power of paradigms as they relate to you and those who are closest to you.

It uses the metaphor of the way crabs behave when they are caught at sea by crab fishermen. When these fisherman head out to sea, they cast out big nets and bring in great quantities of crabs onto the fishing boat where they are placed in great big holding pots. The instinct of most of the crabs is to make a pile in the center of the pot and build a pyramid to the top of the pot. The crabs will wrestle very aggressively to get to the top of the heap, often maiming or killing other crabs along the way, only to find that when they get to the top of the pile they are no closer to freedom than they were at the bottom because they are still too far away from the edge to escape. Occasionally, a crab with a different instinct will start climbing up the side of the pot – which is, of course, the only way to freedom. The pots, over time, get dings and nicks in the sides so the crab is able to get a foothold and carefully scale the side of the pot. When one of the crabs in the heap notices the crab going up the sides, s/he will leave the pile and come over to the side and yank the wayward crab off the wall, back to the bottom of the pot where s/he "belongs."

Have you ever noticed that people tend to behave in very similar ways? Think about it for a moment: Have you ever tried to climb out of your "pot" – that place where you are comfortable and where everyone who knows you best is comfortable with you being? For example, you're reading this book, which means that somewhere along the way you decided that you want something more out of life than you are currently getting.

Let's say, for example, that you are sick and tired of your minimum wage job and want to start your own business. You find a company that has an amazing product that you really love. You already tell everyone you know that they have to try this product, and you learn that the company has a network marketing structure where you can actually earn a very respectable amount of money just by spreading the word about this product and using it yourself (both of which you are already doing). So, you join this company, and you start your own business. Does this scenario sound vaguely familiar? As you start off on your venture, family and friends express their delight at your ingenuity and offer their support and best wishes for your success. As your business begins to take off and you actually start contemplating leaving your day job because you've almost reached the point of replacing your income with your new business, all of a sudden these same relatives and friends subtly begin sabotaging your efforts. Mom worries that maybe the product you are selling isn't safe. A best friend gets angry that you won't go to the bar with him because you have a business presentation and a company webinar to attend. Your spouse or significant other pouts that you are obsessed with the new business and you don't have time for them anymore.

If you are able to withstand the pressure and persist, actually stepping out and quitting your day job because you've more than replaced your salary, the subtly of the sabotage becomes progressively more aggressive – negative comments questioning your sanity in giving up a secure job for a fantasy, belittling your efforts by bringing up past failures, pushing you to neglect your business or risk "hurting their feelings." Eventually, the pressure becomes an all out assault – relationships can even be severed or sorely damaged because of your unwillingness to bend to familial or social pressure.

It's much like the crabs in the above mentioned crab pot. Those closest to you – who say they want the very best for you - see you trying to "get out of the pot" – trying to better yourself in some way, and they do their damnedest to pull you right off the wall, back into your "pot" – where they are comfortable with you – where you (in their mind) belong!

You keep trying, braving their displeasure, ignoring their comments, and they pull out all the stops. They tell you and anyone else who will listen that there is something fishy going on – you're obviously involved in some kind of illegal Ponzi scheme and will likely end up in jail. You try to share what you are learning with them, but, locked on their own perspective, their brains refuse to accept any part of the knowledge you are gaining. They absolutely, passionately refuse to acknowledge how you are changing. To them, your 'assigned' role is cast in stone. At some point you are forced to make a choice – abandon your quest for a better life and once again take your place in the "pot," or, finally get to the uppermost point in your life (the top of the crab pot) and decide to fall outside the pot.

So, to continue the crabbing analogy, what happens when the rare crab makes it to the top of the pot and pulls himself over the edge and lands on the ship's deck? Does the crab fisherman pick him up and throw him back in the pot? No. In reality, the exact opposite happens. The fisherman picks up the crab and throws him back into the ocean, setting him free. The fisherman knows that there is something special in that crab – a survival instinct that is stronger than normal. Such crabs will surely mate and pass this instinct on to their progeny, ensuring the survival of the species for generations of crab fishermen to come!

So, what happens to the person who perseveres and finally makes their way to the top of their personal 'crab pot' and pulls themselves over the edge and falls to the deck? Well, that's where the magic happens – that's when you are free to create whatever big, beautiful life YOU choose. That's when you discover your own power.

Isn't that great? Sadly, however, those who profess to love you the most and want the very best for you will be your most crafty and devious saboteurs – not because they are bad, conniving people, but because they also have paradigms and you have a particular place in those paradigms. Because they are not armed with the awareness that you now have, they act out of habit and instinct and will do whatever they can to derail your efforts.

Commit to surrounding yourself with positive people who support you in your commitment to reach your goals. Now, I am not telling you to abandon your friends and family, but it is critical that you recognize what may happen as you begin to make big changes in your life. Surround yourself with like-minded people. If you have a "crab" in your life trying to "pull you off the wall," grab the lifeline that someone else is holding out for you.

Tool: Inundate Yourself With Your Goal

The key to overcoming all that is holding you back from tremendous success is physically immersing or inundating your senses with your goal. Your instinctive response is to act on physical stimuli. In general, your perception of reality is based on what you take in from the outside world through your five senses. When you immerse your senses in what you want, it drives those images into your subconscious mind where they can move into form through your actions.

The military uses this tool incredibly effectively! In the Corps of Cadet at Virginia Tech (and I'm sure it's the same at other military colleges and academies), the first year is all about being inundated with your goal. As a freshman you are "a nothing, a nobody" and your goal is to get through that first year. The very source of your struggle and humiliation, the upperclassmen, IS the personification of your goal. The upperclassmen bark out orders and get in your face and force you to face fear after fear. At the time you have absolutely no idea how on earth you are going to get through it, but then you look at the people barking out the orders and you realize that they had to endure this at one point in time too, and they got through it. Then, all of a sudden, you make it to the end of the year and you are "turned" and you become a full-fledged member of the Corps. But that's not enough; you can't stagnate; you have to set a new goal so you aspire to higher ranks and more responsibility. It is the same thing with pilot training and basic training – you work your way through one hour at a time, one day at a time, one week at a time, and then, at the end there is a new goal waiting for you. The whole military system of rank continues this process all through your career – there is always the next level to achieve. Your senses are always inundated by that goal.

Here are some examples of how to inundate your senses:

1. **"Photoshop" your bank statement, your sales sheet, your profit and loss report, your income tax return to reflect what you really want it to say.**

2. **Place pictures or post-it-notes on your mirror or around your office. Find pictures on the internet or in magazines that bring the image of your goal to "life."**

3. **Create vision boards (collections of pictures and words that show what you want – Pinterest.com is an excellent place to find all kinds of images for your board – a totally visual, image driven site).**

4. **Use your goal card. Read it, touch it, say it out loud as often as possible.**

5. **Test drive your dream car – involve as many senses as you possibly can (sight, touch, smell, sound).**

For as long as I can remember I have wanted a custom BMW 2-seat convertible. Angie and I were in Florida on a house hunting trip and we passed a BMW dealer in Daytona Beach, so we stopped and talked to a salesperson. I test drove a BMW Z4 convertible that was similar to the one I wanted. We put the top down and took it out on the interstate. Angie took my picture behind the wheel of "my car." I gave the salesman my card and told him we were moving to the area in a couple of months and to call me. We went back to Virginia and every single day I "drove" my Z4. I imagined I was behind the wheel of that Z-4 every time I got in my Honda Civic. In my mind, I saw my new car sitting in my garage. The more I did this, the more surprised I would be when I would go to the garage and see my Honda. Today, my custom built 2012 BMW Z4 resides happily in my garage for real.

6. Make a recording of you reading your vision aloud. Listen to it every morning and every night.
7. Carry a special coin in your pocket to remind yourself of your goal every time you touch it (we have a coin just for this purpose available at www.DebCheslow.com).

You live on three planes of existence simultaneously – spiritual, intellectual and physical. Everything already exists on the spiritual plane, and, as soon as you think of something, it exists on the intellectual plane. Think about that for a second: Once you conceive an idea, you already possess it on two of the three planes of existence. By tapping into your higher, spiritual self you facilitate the manifestation of what you desire on the physical plane. Napoleon Hill said it very well, "We become what we think about most of the time." What you give energy to grows. If you want to achieve the goals you have set for yourself, then "most of the time" you have to have thoughts of you living that life. The more you hold the image of what you want on the screen of your mind, the faster that image will be manifested on the physical plane. And the really cool part is that these techniques can work for anything in your life: your financial condition, your relationships, your career, your health and fitness – ANYTHING!! All the concepts are the same, it's just the application that changes!

5 | AUTOPILOT ENGAGED

In the last chapter, I explained that your self-image is the compilation of all of the habits and beliefs that reside in your subconscious mind – the good, the bad and the ugly. Your self-image operates as a "governor" on your level of accomplishment. Remember that formula for success that I introduced earlier (Success = Burning Desire + Belief + Expectancy + Action)? Your ability to generate the deep down core belief that will allow you to achieve your goal depends on your self-image.

The way your self-image operates can be compared to a thermostat in your home. You set the thermostat to keep the house at a nice, comfortable 70°F. It doesn't really matter what the temperature is outside, the house stays at 70°. I live in Florida, and it can get brutally hot outside during the day. Let's say my son goes outside to play and leaves the front door standing open a little too long. The heat from the outside begins to raise the temperature inside. As soon as the temperature goes above 70°, the thermostat takes over and causes the air conditioning system to turn on. Cool air begins blowing through the ductwork and into the rooms until the temperature in the house comes back down to 70°. It all happens automatically – I don't have to do a thing.

You can also compare your self-image to the way an automatic pilot in a jet works. Basically, the pilot programs the coordinates of the destination into the auto-pilot computer. As the jet flies to its destination, the computer detects deviations from the programmed flight path and makes the necessary corrections to bring the plane back on course. The pilot doesn't have to do a thing – he can get up and walk back into the passenger compartment, have a cup of coffee, go to the bathroom, whatever - the jet essentially flies itself to the programmed destination, much like a three-dimensional version of the cruise control system in your car.

Your self-image regarding your income level, your relationships, your career – pretty much everything in your life – operates in a very similar fashion. Using the diet example once again: You decide you want to release the excess weight on your body, so you start a new nutrition and fitness program (a "diet"), and you follow it to the letter for the first week. You eat exactly the way the plan prescribes, and you work out when and how the plan tells you to. You get to the end of the week, step on the scale, and see you have indeed reduced your weight by a few pounds. The diet works – you have the proof! You may go along like this for weeks or months and continue to drop weight, but, if you haven't addressed your self-image – if you haven't changed the thermostat - if you don't truly believe down deep inside that you will reach and maintain your goal weight, then you will very subtly begin to sabotage your progress. Maybe you justify eating something that is not on your meal plan because you've been so good for so long – surely just this one time won't hurt anything, but then that one time becomes an all day binge or the one day becomes a whole week. Or, perhaps, you justify a "cheat" and then beat yourself up because you were weak. Then you convince yourself that you've blown your diet so you may as well just quit and start over again on Monday. Slowly but surely your weight begins to climb, and, in the sum total of things, you end up back where you started or with a few extra pounds added in just for good measure. Your self-image "thermostat" makes certain that you ultimately end up at your "pre-programmed" weight.

Have you ever wondered why there seem to be certain benchmarks in life that you find incredibly easy to maintain (weight, income, types of social acquaintances, types of personal relationships)? It doesn't matter what you do (or don't do), you just seem to attract the same set of circumstances into your life? That "set point" is the level of belief that is in complete alignment with your self-image, your thermostat setting, and you will always come back to it automatically.

In the case of money, your thermostat (your self-image) is set to one of three settings: You either break even every month (you have enough money to pay your bills and live, but nothing is left over), you fall short every month (you run out of money before your next paycheck arrives) or you have an excess of money every month (more money than month). It doesn't matter how many raises you get (or how many pay cuts you have), you will still end up in whatever scenario your money blueprint is programmed for.

Thought Filters

Interestingly, Deepak Chopra and Wayne Dyer often quote a study that concludes that our minds are bombarded by an average of 65,000 thoughts per day. Yet, the studies also show that the human brain only processes between 2,500 and 3,500 of those thoughts per day, each thought ranging from 12-14 seconds long. According to these same studies, the more focused you are on something, the fewer thoughts you will actually process each day. For instance, elite athletes only process an average of 1,500 thoughts per day because they are so focused on what they are doing in any given moment. Why is it that over 99% of the thoughts that invade our minds each day just "bounce off" and we don't even realize it? It goes back to the self image that resides in our subconscious mind – it actually sets up a "filter" around our conscious mind which only allows thoughts that are consistent with our self-image and our beliefs to pass through.

Let's ponder this for a moment. Have you ever had a friend who had the "Midas touch" - for whom everything they touch turns to gold? If they got fired from a job, they had a better one with a big salary increase and better benefits within a week; if a relationship ended, they found a new partner in a relatively short time who was so much better for them? Yet, you have another friend who struggles and never catches a break – a lost job may mean months on unemployment; a broken relationship results in a carbon copy of a string of previous relationships, just with a different hair color. Why the difference? Yes, there could be differences in skill sets or education level or personality and such that certainly may play a part, but I submit that the overriding reason for the difference is that the first friend has a prosperity conscious self-image and the second friend has a poverty conscious self-image.

The filters that are set around their conscious minds are different, so they are aware of different thoughts. The first friend is absolutely aware of what they need to do to attract a better job or a better relationship and their conscious thoughts and feelings (generated by the self-image in their subconscious mind) are in complete harmony, so they naturally just act in ways that are consistent with getting what they want. The other friend's filter is not letting in the thoughts that would lead them to naturally and effortlessly make the choices they need to produce the desired results. Those thoughts are not in harmony with their self-image, so, although they may KNOW what to do intellectually, they can't quite DO what they know. S/he may force a certain behavior for a time, but, eventually, the self-image wins and the results are back in line with their self-image.

The logical questions then are: "Can I change the filter? Can I change my self-image?" The answer is: "Of course you can!!" You are not forever stuck with your current self-image. When you build big beautiful pictures of everything you want to be, do or have, your subconscious mind has no choice but to accept these thoughts as fact. With repetition over time, you can create a new self-image and thereby create a new physical reality. The process is "simple," but not necessarily easy. That's what this book is all about: I am sharing with you a systemized solution for changing your self-image or your image for your business and achieving success, and, I am giving you all the tools you need to make those changes happen.

> When I went to pilot training, the first hurdle we had to clear was academic in nature – I was very much a student in a classroom again. The first day of my aerodynamics class, our instructor asked for a show of hands of those

> in the room with Aerospace or Aeronautical Engineering degrees. I proudly shot my hand up along with a few others in the room, anxiously awaiting some level of praise for my brilliant foresight when choosing a major in college. Instead, the instructor said, "Take a good look at those people with their hands up. Those are the people who will flunk out of this program." I was shocked! I had never failed a class in my life – obviously he didn't know what he was talking about. He then went on to explain that the people with the engineering degrees would get so wrapped up in the "how" and whether things were accurate from a textbook perspective that they wouldn't be able to accept and learn what he was teaching and would, subsequently, fail. I should have thanked my instructor! He reset my filter and my expectations so that I didn't allow myself to get lost in the how and in the minute details. I allowed myself to be teachable and trainable and stayed focused on my vision! I actually ended up graduating #1 academically in my pilot training class, but that only happened because I was told that I would fail, and I allowed my filter to change as a result of that challenge.

Since your subconscious mind has no choice but to accept what you think, you have to nourish it with healthy and encouraging information. If you don't make a conscious effort to take control of your self-destructive thoughts, they'll take over and rot out the positive ones, leaving your life a crumbling mess. Your subconscious mind is incredibly powerful. Thoughts become things. That's not just "woo-woo" nonsense; it is actually true – you think a thought in your conscious mind and impress that thought on your subconscious mind over and over again. The feelings associated with the thought cause you to act in ways that are consistent with the thought, thus bringing about the result. If you mistakenly focus on what you don't want, you will bring about those results just as readily as the things you do want. So, let's look at a monster tool that will help you re-program your auto-pilot and change your self-image.

Tool: Imagineering

"Imagineering" is a combination of the words "imagination" and "engineering." The term was coined by Alcoa in the 1940's, but is more popularly associated with Walt Disney. Walt Disney used Imagineering to transform a useless swamp in the middle of Florida into the vacation mecca of the world. The idea behind imagineering is to take the limits off your thoughts about what is possible and to let your imagination go where logic says it cannot – to allow yourself to dream again like you did when you were a child.

You can use the concept of imagineering in any area of your life that you want to improve. Take the statement that you wrote on your goal card and spend 30 minutes imagineering your desired end result each day – 15 minutes of written imagineering and then 15 minutes spent just thinking about what you wrote and FEELING it. Just let go of logic and circumstantial constraints and WRITE! No one is going to read it but you – it's an absolutely private exchange between you and the universe. No one is checking your spelling, grammar or punctuation, so let it flow. It can be difficult in the beginning – people get so used to being "logical" and "rational" that taking the lid off and dreaming BIG can be really hard!!

DREAM BIG anyway!!! Start each imagineering session with *"I am so happy and grateful now that..."* and let the details of your ideal life flow out onto the paper as if they are already facts in your life right now. Look back at how you responded to the questions at the end of Chapter 2 to get you started. Don't worry about HOW it will happen – that's not your concern at this point. The most important part is to only give energy to what you WANT – give no thought to what you don't want (for instance, write "I am so happy and grateful now that I am earning $500,000 per year doing exactly what I love and that money comes to me effortlessly from multiple sources on a continuous basis" rather than "I am so happy and grateful now that I am not in debt anymore"). The subconscious mind only processes images; it doesn't hear verbs, adverbs, qualifiers, etc. If you think "not in debt anymore" your subconscious mind only processes "debt" and has a very clear image of bills and debt and an empty bank account! Remember, we think in pictures!! So, what do you think you'll be attracting into your life in this case? That's right. DEBT!

Now, imagine that you have already achieved your goal. Detail in writing how you FEEL now that you have achieved what you want – become emotionally involved in your vision. That is how you change the auto-pilot - your self-image – by getting emotionally involved with the IMAGES associated with what you want.

Again, we know that some people have difficulty with the concept of imagineering in the beginning. You know you want a change, but it's been so long since you allowed yourself to dream beyond the here and now that you have trouble getting started. Just begin with *"I am so happy and grateful now that..."* and then take some piece of the life that will manifest when you attain your goal, and write about that small piece – maybe it's the joy you feel the first time you realize that you have money left over in your checking account when the next pay day comes; maybe it's the pride you feel every time you look down at that championship ring on your finger; maybe it's the look in your wife's eyes when you come home with flowers and theater tickets "just because"; maybe it's looking at your bank statement and realizing you have just crossed the $1,000,000 mark in your account balance. Just start writing about SOMETHING. Over time the words will begin to flow from your mind onto the paper and intuition will lead you to envision things you want to be, do or have in other areas of your life. Soon there will be no stopping you – you'll be a dream machine!!

What you write about is entirely up to you, and it can change from day to day; just let it flow. Details will come into your mind that you never thought of before (that is intuition speaking). When you have experienced a burst of intuition, just allow the words to pour from your pen onto the paper. When you have finished, sit back and close your eyes and spend 15 minutes thinking about that new intuitive detail that you just wrote about. Sometimes when you are spending time reflecting on what you wrote you will experience a "vision" about some new facet of what your life will be – again, this is intuition speaking. So, the next time you imagineer, write about that vision. This is a very creative process!

One important note – I have tested this process over and over again and I can tell you from personal experience that typing on a keyboard is not the same as taking a pen and paper and kicking it old school. You will not get the same mind-body connection when you are typing into a word processing document as you will when you are writing with a pen and paper. Actual writing on a sheet of paper causes your mind to think; thinking evokes images; those images cause feelings in your subconscious mind; the feelings move you into action and the action causes a re-action (a result). Then you can analyze your result, see if it is in line with what you want and make adjustments in your imagineering to start the process all over again. The people I have worked with (including myself) who have tried it both ways (computer and pen/paper) have achieved significantly better and faster results with good old pen and paper.

Typing into a computer and writing by hand each stimulate a different level of brain activation. In extremely simplistic terms, typing on a keyboard activates only eight neural pathways, while writing long-hand, regardless of the language you are writing in, activates over 10,000 neural pathways – you literally feel the thought when you write long hand!

Similarly, just thinking about what you want isn't good enough either because you can't control your logic when you just think about something. There will constantly be interruptions as logic wants to know, "Well how on earth are you going to do that?" Remember, the HOW is not important right now, just that you want it, and writing allows you to circumvent logic!

Let's look at some examples of good and bad imagineering:

Good Example

I am so happy and grateful now that I live an incredibly abundant life, overflowing with love, joy, happiness, success, great health and complete financial independence. I live in my dream house with my soul mate surrounded by luxury and grandeur at each and every turn. I spend freely on myself and others and love the feeling of helping someone in need. Money comes to me in increasing quantities through multiple sources on a continuous basis.

Bad Example

I am so happy and grateful now that I am out of debt and can finally pay my bills. I am making so much more money which means that I can afford to fix my car when it breaks down. It is great to be able to go out with the guys on Friday night and have a beer without bouncing a check. My wife doesn't yell at me about how much money I spend anymore and that is really nice...

Can you see the difference between these two paragraphs? The first example relates life in all positive terms, while the second example is filled with imagery of what used to be – the debt, the empty bank account, the bounced checks, the arguments. The subconscious mind processes images, so it doesn't realize that you are talking about what used to be or what you are so glad is gone – it processes what you write – debt, broken cars, bounced checks, arguments, etc. – and will do everything possible to make sure you get more of those things!!

Imagineering is a process - and it can be pretty darned frustrating at times. You don't just start writing one day and wake up the next day with a million dollars in your bank account. It's an evolution. Changing the habits that have been with you for decades is hard work!! The more junk that's been heaped on you over those decades, the harder it is, but there is nothing better than when you wake up one day and realize that you really have changed and that life is better and you really do need a telescope to see how far you've come.

Although imagineering is a creative process and you have ultimate control over what you write about, it does have "rules"; there are standards and you have to have the discipline to follow them. The biggest and most important standard is that you must do it every single day. In Chapter 6 I recap a NASA study that found it takes 30 days for a new habit to form, so that is one reason to do this daily. The other reason is that, when you visualize your goal, you have a markedly better chance of achieving it, so the more often you do it, the better.

Here is a story that illustrates this point very well: Back in 1988, an oil tycoon named Patrick Taylor was asked to speak to a group of 183 7th and 8th grade students from a school in a very poor parish in Louisiana. At this particular school, 84% of the kids dropped out of high school. Mr. Taylor told these children that if they stayed in school, stayed out of trouble, and completed a college preparatory high school curriculum with a B average he would see to it that each of them received a college education, at no cost to them or their families. Of course, the response was overwhelming – the children and their parents were stunned and so happy.

However, Mr. Taylor was a student of human behavior and knew that excitement would fade over time and the kids' conditioning (college was completely outside their experience or that of their families) would take over and his offer would soon be forgotten (remember, welfarekids tend to grow up to be welfare adults), so he went a step further. He arranged a "field trip" to a local college where each of these kids buddied up with a college student and shadowed them for a day. They went to classes and hung out in the dormitories and ate in the dining hall and played football on the quad and really lived the life of a college student for a day. Through this exercise he created a picture, a visual image for the kids to call upon, but he knew that, over time, this too would fade. After all, how many kids want to be an astronaut after going on a field trip to the Kennedy Space Center or a race car driver after visiting a race track? Lots of them! But how many actually become astronauts or race car drivers? Not many. The vision fades.

So Taylor went yet a step further. He made Imagineering a part of each child's life. For the next four years, the kids were allowed 15 minutes during their school day to visualize their college experience. Nothing else changed in that school – same teachers, same curriculum, same 84% drop out rate, but, when the time came for this group of former underachievers to graduate, 86% of them did so and went on to college. That's remarkable!

IMAGINEERING: Summing it up

- **IMAGINEER EVERY DAY!**
- **Buy a cool notebook or binder and a nice pen that is dedicated just for your imagineering – make this time special for YOU;**
- **Enjoy 15 minutes of freeflow writing and then 15 minutes visualizing what you wrote in a relaxed state;**
- **Start with** *"I am so happy and grateful now that....."*

- **Describe your ideal life – whatever you feel like writing about that day - in the present tense as if it were already a fact;**
- **Only discuss what you want; do not give ANY energy to what you don't want.**

Imagineering is one of those things that is easy to put off or let go by the wayside when time is tight. Make imagineering a priority – better yet, make it a HABIT!! Hard schedule it into your calendar if you have to. Don't just make a half-hearted commitment here! It takes discipline. Imagineering is the single most effective way to change your self-image, but you have to do it every, single day! There have been days when I stagger into the house after a non-stop 16 hour day and all I want to do is fall into bed, but I still take those 30 minutes and imagineer – after all this time, I still do it EVERY SINGLE DAY!! Even when you have made it into a habit there is something to be aware of. It can be easy to forget where you started and to allow logic to make you question whether it is really worth all the time and effort. Left unchecked, logic will have you slipping back into your old habits. So be vigilant! Imagineer every day no matter what; make it so much a part of your life that it is like brushing your teeth and you can't even conceive of not doing it.

> I have used imagineering to achieve goals all my life – long before I knew anything about what it was called or the science behind the process. I remember a time during Pilot Training when I was soloing in a T-37 Trainer. My perception was that each flight was getting better and better,

yet I wasn't getting passing grades in landing the plane. Suddenly and unbelievably, I found myself in a position where all my hopes and aspirations of becoming an Air Force pilot were on the line and could all be over in three days! I went home that night and sat in my favorite chair, but rather than sit there and dwell on the end of the world, I closed my eyes and focused on sticking the landing in my plane over and over again – perfect landing after perfect landing. I probably landed my trainer 1,000 times in my mind that night. The next day when I got in the cockpit, I flew my ride and stuck the landing and then started breathing again. What do you think the outcome would have been if instead I had envisioned all the bad stuff that would have happened if I had failed my ride?

6 | Manuveuring Through the Storm

One of my favorite quotes is by Albert Einstein: "Insanity is doing the same thing over and over again, expecting a different result." According to that definition, there are a lot of insane people walking around out there; are *you* one of them? If you want to change your life then you have to *change* your life. The problem is that most people are paralyzed by the prospect of change; paralyzed by fear. Change is hard; it's scary, but in order to be successful in any endeavor, you must have the courage and the discipline to identify and change what isn't working. Remember, courage is not the absence of fear; it's stepping into action in spite of the fear you feel.

In order to make any type of permanent change, it is critical that you examine the habitual patterns of behavior that are keeping you from achieving the results you want (unproductive habits) and then take measures to change them.

CHANGING HABITS AND PARADIGMS

The subconscious mind expresses itself through your feelings which lead to your actions and behavior, which produce results (sorry, but you have to take action to produce results – anything else is just wishful thinking). When you string a bunch of these goal-driven actions together you can begin to see how your reality will also change. By learning to apply this knowledge to your life, you'll realize that you can have whatever you want in life.

So, let's break it down. You think thoughts in your conscious mind – you have the ability to choose those thoughts, to accept the thoughts you like and to reject the ones you don't like. The thoughts that you ultimately think generate feelings in your subconscious mind, and you can't control those feelings – they just reach up and grab you. You can't walk down the street thinking about the day your dog died and have a skip in your step and a smile on your face. Feelings, not thoughts, move you into action. You can override your feelings short-term and force action (that's called behavior modification), but, as soon as you are not consciously thinking about what you are doing, you will revert back to acting based on your feelings (your habits). And, of course, action is the only thing that will produce results – anyone who says differently is selling something!!

Thoughts ➡ *Feelings* ➡ *Actions* ➡ *Results*

Let's examine this further. What do most people spend the majority of their time thinking about? What do you spend most of your time thinking about? I contend that the vast majority of people spend an overwhelming majority of their time focusing their thoughts on their current situation, on the current results – the current job, that annoying coworker, the fight they had with their spouse this morning, the game they lost last week, the fact that they are 50 pounds overweight, that there is only $25 left in the bank account and payday is a week away, and so on. Well, if that is what you are thinking about, and thoughts lead to feelings, which drive your actions, which produce your results, what are you going to get more of? More of the same old results, right? It's a never ending cycle! That, my friend, is a mid-life crisis. That is a relationship that is stuck in a rut. That is a business that has stopped growing. You can't expect to create something big and beautiful and beyond anything you've done before if you keep your mind cluttered with all the same old dusty thoughts!!

> *For 11 years I had what I considered to be an idyllic marriage – my husband and I were perfectly compatible, agreed on almost everything, had only three fights during those 11 years and generally led a charmed, wonderful existence. So, you can imagine my surprise as we were making Christmas cookies, watching our girls play in the snow in the front yard that day in December 2002 when he told me he wanted a divorce. He had fallen in love with someone and he was leaving me, our daughters and our life to build a new life with that person. I was numb, absolutely shocked. I tried to convince him that we could work out any issues, but he said "No;" he wanted out. Ten days later he and all his belongings were gone. I thought my life was over – that my reason for living had walked out the door, and thus began the grandest 8 year*

pity-party the world has ever seen! I couldn't let go of my anger over what "he'd done to me," my grief over my loss, my jealousy that he was able to move on with his life so seamlessly while I was just cast aside, marking time, stuck in a past I wasn't ready to release. It wasn't until I started studying this material that I came to the conclusion that I was my own jailor. I was the only one standing in the way of my future happiness. Becoming an unemotional, logical hermit was not "punishing" my ex-husband, but it was certainly punishing my children, and it was robbing me of the wonderful life I was destined for.

Once I released the negative thoughts of my circumstances and started envisioning my life with new possibilities and new love, everything turned around on a dime – literally within a matter of a few months! I attracted my true soul mate, who makes my heart sing each and every day. I turned around a whole myriad of health problems. I earned my black belt in karate. I redirected my consulting business operations to focus on what I love doing. So you see, everything really does happen for a reason. Once I stopped dwelling on my limiting thoughts, the process followed true to form and my results were better than I could have possibly hoped!

Let's take the Thoughts-Feelings-Actions-Results process a step further. It is ingrained in the majority of people from a very early age that in order to learn you have to accumulate "information." Learning means reading books and going to classes, trainings, seminars and stuffing volumes of information in your brain, right? People don't really "study" books anymore. It's as if the more books you have on your bookshelves the smarter you must be. And, heaven forbid, you ever go back and read a book a second time – why would you do that? You've already read it! That's the traditional educational model – read the book, regurgitate the information, pass the test, put the book on the shelf, move on to the next book. You end up with all this information (in your conscious mind), but you never put it into action in any meaningful way because you have done nothing to address the habits (in your subconscious mind) that will ultimately drive your consistent action and create your improved results.

To illustrate my point, let's use the example of a training workshop. Your company sends you to a week-long workshop and you receive some amazing information – things that you just KNOW are going to make you a shining star in your organization – you have the keys to the kingdom in that training binder in your suitcase and you're excited! Monday morning rolls around and you head into the office with your binder and you just can't wait to start implementing what you've learned. You get to your desk, flip on your computer and there are 500 new emails in your inbox; the message light is flashing on your phone; there is a stack of paper a foot tall in your inbox; and there is an urgent message in the center of your blotter that your boss needs to see you as soon as you get in. So you spend all day Monday returning phone calls and emails, putting out fires with your boss, and managing paperwork. You end up leaving the office without even opening your training binder. Tuesday is much the same. Wednesday, you actually get a little bit of a reprieve, so you take out the binder and make a few notes on your to-do list, but then there is another crisis that eats up Thursday and Friday. The week is over and you haven't had the time to implement even one thing that you learned at the workshop. Monday morning brings more emails, more phone messages, more crises. Six months later you run across your magical training binder at the bottom of a pile on the corner of your desk and you wistfully think, "What a shame. That workshop didn't work at all." Then you head off to another training seminar and the cycle begins anew; more time, more money, and nothing ever changes.

You see, training provides valuable information, but all that information is locked in your conscious mind. In order to bridge the "Information-Action Gap" you must tackle the habits that are keeping you stuck in place so that you can actually do what you know how to do! So, to give a more accurate picture of reality, let's restructure the process:

Information ➡ Habits ➡ Action ➡ Results

In order to put the information that you have in your conscious mind into action you have to change your habits – anything else is just behavior modification and the results will only be short-term in duration.

The next logical question then is: "How do I change the habits that are keeping me stuck?" Well, there are only two ways to change a habit (or a collection of habits - a paradigm):

REMARKABLE COURAGE

1. Emotional Impact
2. Spaced Repetition of an Idea

Emotional impact events work fast, but you can't predict them and they are usually negative. Think about the sudden death of a loved one – the person was here just this morning and then WHAM! – s/he is gone. There is an emotional impact from an event like that – pain, sadness, grief, possibly guilt or regret. Such an event can change the way you view your world and your place in it.

> When I was in high school I had nearly perfect grades. I routinely got perfect scores on tests, papers, reports, and the like. Now, it was not uncommon for kids to compare grades while the teacher was handing papers back, and I was always proud to share my score. I never did this to brag – I never even considered it might be construed by other kids as bragging, but one day a teacher was handing back a test and I got a 100%. I turned to my friend behind me and asked what she got. She looked at me and said, "Look Debbie, I know you got 100. You ALWAYS get 100, but you know what? We're all just sick of you bragging about it!" It stung me to my core! There was emotional impact. From that moment on, I never shared my grades again. I never shared my accomplishments. I got embarrassed when I was recognized for anything, worried that people would think I

was bragging. I went through my entire adult life like this. A few months ago we were having a staff meeting and our Executive Marketing Director got really exasperated with me. She was working on some promotional materials for the company and wanted to highlight the fact that I had been an instructor pilot and that I was a karate black belt and the like and I kept saying that it was irrelevant. I kept resisting her. Finally she looked at me and said, "Deb, I feel like a boxer in the ring with one hand tied behind my back. I have everything I need to win this thing but half my weapons are useless! People need to hear your story. It's important. It's inspiring. It will HELP them – isn't that what this company is all about?" It was a few days later when I realized what I was doing – my paradigm was to hide my achievements. I was handicapping my company with my "humility," and it all went back to an emotional impact moment - to a snarky comment that some 14 year old girl made to me 3-1/2 decades ago!!

Spaced repetition of an idea, on the other hand, can be a slow process, but it works! It requires diligent, persistent effort, but anyone can do it and it can be a truly wonderful, positive process.

You've already done a great deal of introspection throughout this book so far, but here is another place where YOU have to get

REMARKABLE COURAGE

real with YOU, because nothing else in this book is going to help you make a LASTING change until you do.

Sit down and relax and really think about how you go through your day. What are the things that you are doing habitually (without conscious thought) that are holding you back from achieving your desired goals? Do you spend money carelessly or charge purchases to credit cards that you can't pay back in full each month? Do you habitually act in a reckless manner with your financial obligations? Do you put off actions that could help you get out of your current situation until "tomorrow?"

Write down the 3 most prevalent habits that are holding you back.

1. _____
_____
_____

2. _____
_____
_____

3. _____
_____
_____

The biggest part of getting what you want in life lies in knowing what you have to give up in order to achieve it. Now, I don't mean this from a "lack and limitation" perspective, but rather from the perspective of giving up something of a lower nature to gain something of a higher nature. So now that you have identified what's holding you back, know that those are the things you need to give up.

Nature abhors a vacuum. If you give up something, it leaves a vacuum – a hole – and the natural order of things is to fill the vacuum as quickly as possible. As human beings, this basic truth holds again and again: if you don't consciously replace a negative habit with a positive habit it will be replaced with a new negative habit, subconsciously. So, now that you have identified the habits that are holding you back, you need to flip each one on its ear and turn it into a positive.

In the space provided, turn each of your negative habits into positives:

1. _____

_____

_____

2. _____

_____

_____

REMARKABLE COURAGE

3. _____
_____
_____

WHAT DOES NASA HAVE TO DO WITH MY HABITS?

Let's talk about the science of changing a habit for a moment. Research has shown that it takes at least 30 days to begin to form a new habit. In fact, one of these research studies is an incredible illustration of the physiological connection between time and "habits." Back in the early days of the space program, NASA designed an experiment to determine the physiological and psychological effects of the spatial disorientation the astronauts would experience in the weightless environment of space.

NASA needed to know if the environment of space would have some unexpected negative consequences that would endanger the astronauts or their mission. Would they black out and be unable to function? Would they experience some psychotic event that would leave them incapacitated? NASA scientists outfitted each of the astronauts with a pair of convex goggles which flipped everything in their field of vision 180 degrees. In other words, their world was literally turned upside down. The astronauts had to wear the goggles 24 hours a day, 7 days per week—even when they were asleep.

Although they experienced physical symptoms of anxiety and stress initially – elevated blood pressure, respiration and other vital signs - they gradually adapted to their new "realities." On the 26th day of the experiment, something amazing happened for one of the astronauts. His world turned right-side up again even though he continued to wear the goggles 24 hours a day. Between days 26-30, the same thing happened for each of the remaining astronauts. What the scientists discovered is that, after 26-30 days of this continuous stream of new input, the astronauts' brains actually created neural pathways that "rewired" their brains to see their worlds normally again.

Then NASA repeated the experiment with a slight change. This time some of the astronauts took the goggles off for a short period of time partway through the experiment. When they put the goggles back on and left them on until the 30th day, their worlds were still upside down, but when they continued on, at 26-30 consecutive days wearing the goggles, the same thing happened – everything was suddenly right side up again. What the scientists discovered from these experiments is that the brain requires approximately 30 uninterrupted days for new neural connections to form – for new habits to form.

In order to change a habit, it is crucial that you put systems in place to insure you follow the new behavior you have chosen. Otherwise, without thinking you will revert to the old behavior! After 30 days of conscious, intentional, deliberate thought and effort it gets easier and easier, and by 90 days it is very much a part of who you are – a new habit; only this time it's one that is serving you and moving you toward your goals. Then you can start the whole process over to change additional bad habits!

It's important to understand that it's not good enough to just decide to break a bad habit. Once the bad habit is gone, what is it replaced with? Remember, nature abhors a vacuum and releasing a bad habit leaves a void that will be filled with something. So, if you do not consciously replace a habit that it not serving you with one that will, then I can guarantee you that the void will be filled by another "bad" habit because it's easier. Think about people who quit smoking and then gain a bunch of weight. They decide they are going to quit smoking and that is great, but then they replace that habit of bringing the cigarette up to their mouth with the habit of bringing food up to their mouth!! My mother had been a heavy smoker for 50 years when she had a health scare which provided the emotional impact she needed to quit smoking. She quit cold turkey – no patch, no tapering; she just quit; however, she knew the statistics and she knew that she was likely to gain weight when she quit, so she started carrying sugar-free hard candies with her wherever she went. When she would get the urge for a cigarette, she would pop a candy in her mouth instead. She purposefully replaced her smoking habit with a much more innocuous habit and she didn't gain weight either!

The 4 Stages of Learning

At this point, I'd like to introduce you to some information that will help you understand where you are in the process of habitualizing behavior. There are four stages of learning:

1. **Unconscious Incompetence;**
2. **Conscious Incompetence;**
3. **Conscious Competence; and**
4. **Unconscious Competence.**

At the first stage, *unconscious incompetence*, you don't know something, and, furthermore, you don't even know that you don't know it. At the *conscious incompetence* stage, you are aware that you don't know something. At the next stage, *conscious competence*, you are able to do something if you consciously apply yourself. At the final stage of learning, *unconscious competence*, you have mastered a concept or task to the point that you just do it without thinking about it; in other words it has become a habit.

Think about a child's experience learning to ride a bicycle. When a child is a baby or a toddler he is unconsciously incompetent at riding a bicycle – he doesn't even know that there is such a thing as a bicycle, much less that he can't ride one. Then one day the child is playing in the front yard and one of the neighborhood kids rides by on a bicycle and the child becomes aware of this thing called a bike. So Mom and Dad go to the store and buy the child a nice shiny bike with training wheels and sit him on the seat, and the child just sits there. He is consciously incompetent at riding a bike – he knows that the other kids were sitting on their bicycle and it was moving, and he also knows he can't do it. Then Mom and Dad show the child which way to push the pedals and how to steer and how to use the brakes. If the child thinks very hard and tries with all his might, he is able to make the bike move. He has to concentrate on what he is doing in each step, and, if he loses his focus, he either stops or starts rolling backwards or falls off. The child has become a conscious competent at riding a bike. He can do it, but only when focusing on the task. With practice and time, the child becomes so proficient at operating the bicycle that he no longer has to think about it. He just jumps on and goes – he is unconsciously competent at riding a bicycle – the steps needed to operate the bike have become habitual.

This book is moving you through these stages of learning chapter by chapter. There was a time when you didn't know what you didn't know – you were unaware of this material and you didn't know how to use it (unconscious incompetent). Then maybe you went to one of my seminars or read another book or saw a movie that made you aware of the existence of this material, but you didn't quite grasp how to apply it (conscious incompetent). So you picked up this book and you started learning more and more. Now, when you are thinking about it, you can keep your goal in your mind and think about what you want and attract awesome things into your life; however, when you're not consciously thinking about applying the material, you may still find yourself going negative (conscious competence). My goal is to get you to the place where I am – where you apply this material to your life without even thinking about it. When a negative thought enters my mind, I habitually flip it to a positive thought, or dismiss it entirely and replace it with a positive thought (unconscious competent).

So get excited!! You are already at the 3rd Stage of Learning and on your way to the 4th! Think of all the millions – maybe billions – of people on this planet who are wandering around unconsciously incompetent in these concepts – just letting life happen to them. It's so sad! You, however, are CREATING your reality and that is a thrilling, wonderful place to be!

Tool: Accountability Agreements

Changing habitual actions is a fantastic place to use an accountability partner. Back in 1993, a study was conducted at Brigham Young University related to goal achievement. The study found that the probability of achieving a particular goal was associated with the statements a person made about the goal. People who said, "That's a good idea" had a 10% chance. Those who said, "I'll do it," had a 25% chance of reaching their goal. Those who put a date by which they planned to achieve their goal had a 40% chance of doing so. Those who developed a specific plan for reaching their goal had a 50% chance of getting there. Those who committed to someone else that they would accomplish their goal had a 60% chance of making it. But those people who committed to someone else and also committed to sharing their progress at regular intervals had a 95% chance of reaching their goal!!

The power of accountability is incredible and, as you can see, greatly increases your chances of doing what you say you are going to do. This is one reason why it is so important to have a coach or a mentor. How many times have you made a commitment to yourself, but then let yourself off the hook when the going gets tough? It is next to impossible for you to see past your own logic! Does that mean you need to run to the phone and hire a coach? Not necessarily, but finding an "accountability partner" can be one of the most powerful things you can do if you REALLY want to reach a particular goal. I like a quote I read: "Accountability bridges the gap between intention and results!"

Finding the right accountability partner is critical. It should be someone you can trust with your dreams and someone whose opinion you value and for whom you have great respect (in other words it would hurt to let them down). In some cases it could be a best friend or a spouse (sometimes, however, those people could be the very WORST accountability partners – remember the crab pot story). You could also choose a business colleague, a networking associate, etc. You have to be willing to commit to what you wish to be held accountable for and to sharing your progress at regular intervals, and they have to be willing to hold your feet to the fire and carry through with the consequence if need be.

Your Accountability Partner must agree to request progress reports from you at an agreed upon interval of time. If left to you to provide these updates, you would likely forget all about them – this is your paradigm's way of insuring that you stay stuck right where you are.

Accountability without consequence is meaningless. Some may say, "Well, the consequence for not meeting my deadline is that I don't reach my goal," and that's true, but as human beings we are pleasure seekers and pain avoiders. It is my experience that accountability contracts that have a clearly defined consequence for non-performance work best. The consequence needs to be a source of more pain than the tasks associated with what you're being held accountable for.

If you have a goal that you REALLY want to accomplish, carefully select an accountability partner, define and date what you are being held accountable for and devise a consequence for non-performance that will cause more pain than whatever you have to do to meet your deadline. A sample Accountability Agreement is shown on the following page that will get you started (and is available for download at www.DebCheslow.com).

ACCOUNTABILITY AGREEMENT

THIS AGREEMENT is entered into by and between _____

("Participant") and _____
("Accountability Partner") this _____
day of _____, 20____. In consideration of the mutual promises made in this agreement, the parties agree as follows:

1. Participant pledges and agrees to perform the action detailed below by the date specified and to be accountable to the Accountability Partner for progress reports at _____ intervals.

Action Step   Due Date

_____   _____

2. Accountability Partner agrees to hold Participant accountable for the performance of the action listed above by the specified date and to request progress reports from Participant at the interval detailed above.

3. Failure of Participant to comply with request for progress reports by Accountability Partner in a timely manner constitutes a breach of this Agreement; however, failure to meet incremental action plans that may be agreed upon between progress report updates does not constitute a breach of the Agreement, per se.

4. Both Participant and Accountability Partner acknowledge that accountability without consequence is meaningless and agree to the following consequence for non-performance. Accountability Partner accepts the responsibility for enforcing the consequence.

REMARKABLE COURAGE

Consequence for Non-Performance

_____
_____
_____
_____
_____
_____

My signature indicates my understanding and acceptance of this Agreement.

_____   _____
Participant   **Accountability Partner**

_____   _____
Printed Name   **Printed Name**

_____   _____
Signature   **Signature**

_____   _____
Date   **Date**

7 | NO PAIN, NO GAIN: HOW BAD DO YOU WANT IT?

One of my favorite hobbies is weightlifting. I enjoy the feeling of challenging my body to see what it is capable of – to see how far I can go. There is a saying, "No Pain, No Gain" and I can tell you that in the middle of a lifting set, there is PAIN – a lot of pain, but the thrill comes from pushing through the discomfort to achieve something you weren't sure you could accomplish. One of the things that every athlete has to guard against is complacency – getting to a certain level that is challenging but not pushing through to the next level. That's when performance plateaus set in. I know in my own experience with weightlifting, I have occasionally gotten to the point where I was lifting an impressive amount of weight (well, I was impressed anyway), and I would just stay at that weigh long after I COULD have lifted more. Businesses and organizations operate the same way. They achieve a certain level of success that is easy to maintain and they just stay there when they are capable of achieving so much more! The same happens with people and their income, their physical fitness, their relationships, their careers. Why does this happen?

You're Going to Make Me Learn Physics Now?

Inertia is a funny thing – a body at rest tends to remain at rest; a body in motion tends to remain in motion. The trick is to start somewhere. You have identified your goal, so look at where you are and then have the courage to take a baby step. Choose one thing that you can do right now that will move you forward in the right direction. Go as far as you can see and do what you can do right now. Once you do that thing, then you'll be able to see what you need to do from there. Think of the journey to your goal like walking up a long flight of stairs. You can't go from the bottom step to the top in one bound. You take one step and then the next – sometimes you can skip a step (I call that a quantum leap), but, in general, you take one step and then the next and then the next.

We already covered how your identity is strongly influenced by the environment you grew up in and the people you were surrounded by. You learned "right" and "wrong," what you "should" and "shouldn't" do, what is "true" and what is "untrue." This information lives deep inside you and controls your behavior behind the scenes when you are not consciously thinking about doing something else. Consequently, when you are purposing some big new dream, your conscious actions often times don't align with your subconscious conditioning.

Think about it for a second: how much easier is it for you to believe "I can't" than it is for you to believe "I can?" We live in a world where limitations are emphasized much more than potential, so we have to make a conscious, deliberate effort to reinforce the positive and override the negative conversations from our internal and external environments. I work very hard at keeping myself in a positive head space—I do not let external stimuli (people, the media, the guy who just cut me off on the highway) determine my state of mind. I make a determined effort to keep all of my thoughts on a positive, creative plane—and, as a result, I generally feel pretty good, which manifests my actions and produces the kind of results I want. Am I perfect? Hell No! There are days when I wake up on the very wrong side of the bed, and it seems as if there is nothing positive to focus on. But that's the beauty of being surrounded by other people who "get it!" When I am in a funk about something, I have someone around to snap me back to reality—and it does work! The fact is, it is impossible to maintain a positive attitude while you are thinking negative thoughts and vice-versa.

What is your attitude toward yourself, your career, your team, your business, your relationships, and your life in general? Good? Bad? Indifferent? Does it match that of your parents or siblings? The thoughts you think throughout the day are like a vacuum cleaner. Once you begin to feel a certain way it's as if you've been sucked into a "thought vortex" that just keeps sucking in like thoughts. Think about it: When you are down on yourself about something, don't you find yourself finding more and more things to berate yourself about? Negative thoughts like, "I can't do it." "I'm not good enough." "No one likes me." – otherwise known as a pity party.

CREATE OR DISINTEGRATE

There is a basic law of nature that states that nothing stands still - we are either "creating" or are we "disintegrating." In other words, we are either living our lives in ways that move us forward or in ways that move us backwards. Disintegration occurs when

we let life happen to us – when we take our eyes off our goal and allow ourselves to be held prisoner by our circumstances, our self-imposed limitations, our fears, our doubts and worries – when we don't have anything that we're working toward that inspires us. Disintegration is the ultimate manifestation of anxiety and dis-ease (a body not at ease).

Creation, on the other hand, results from knowledge, from understanding based on study and the belief that you can ultimately influence the direction of your life. Creation comes from a state of mental wellbeing and being at ease. Creation occurs when you are focusing your attention on building something – your business, a relationship, your faith, etc. You have a goal that you are moving towards – something that is big and beyond anything you have ever done before. You have no idea how you are going to achieve it, but you have a burning desire for its attainment and you work every day on taking the next baby step (or quantum leap, depending on the day) toward it.

In fact, every single minute of every single day you face a choice: live or slowly die. That sounds harsh, but if you think about it, you will see the truth in it. Every day you literally trade your life for what you do. Put in those terms, you have to ask yourself: Is my job (relationship, finances, spiritual awareness, personal life – whatever conditions or circumstances you have in your life) worth trading my life for? If you can honestly say "YES," then congratulations! However, if you answer "No" or "Yes, BUT," then you probably find yourself feeling dissatisfied a good amount of the time. Here's the good news: Dissatisfaction is the higher side of your personality seeking expansion and fuller expression. Dissatisfaction itself IS a creative state – it is urging you onward and upward. At the happiest points in my life I can honestly say that I was incredibly happy and fulfilled, but never "satisfied."

Energy and Attraction

I spend a lot of time with clients helping them to understand one very important truth – you become what you think about. If you are thinking about what you want in life, I can assure you that you will attract it; however, if you are spending time thinking about what you DON'T want, I can assure you with just as great a level of certainty that you will keep getting more of THAT! The easiest way to explain it is to compare yourself to a magnet and realize that your thoughts and your feelings control your polarity – whether you are attracting positive to you or negative.

At your most basic state you are just a large mass of energy and so is everything else – the chair you are sitting in, the keyboard I am typing on, the sandwich you had for lunch – all just a big mass of energy molecules moving at varying amplitudes of vibration - the more solid an object, the faster and narrower the vibratory rate. Energy fields have a "charge" – an attractive force, and since you are essentially an energy field, YOU have a positive or negative charge too. Your thoughts and feelings control that charge – the amplitude of vibration at which your body is moving.

When you are feeling happy and like everything is hitting on all eight cylinders, do you ever stop to notice that it seems like nothing can go wrong – more good just seems to come your way? You wake up feeling awesome and the kids and spouse are more cooperative and accommodating, it seems there is less traffic on the drive to work, your boss gives you a great compliment on the presentation you made the day before, and so on – it's just a great day! The same can be said when you are having a bad day. You get out of bed, stub your toe on the bed frame, get shampoo in your eyes, burn the toast, leave the house late because Sally refused to get dressed, get stuck in a huge traffic snarl and get yelled at by your boss because you're late to work, and so on.

The best way I know of to control your vibratory rate is to monitor how you are feeling. FEELING is the word we use to describe the conscious awareness of our vibratory state. So, if you find yourself feeling bad, do whatever you can to turn your mood around because your low vibratory rate resulting from your bad mood is attracting all kinds of nastiness to you. In fact, germs vibrate on a very low level, so if you stay positive the majority of the time and vibrate high, it's like oil and water – germs, viruses, bacteria, etc. can't survive in a "positive" environment. It's very interesting – I am in contact with people all the time - as a speaker, I'm constantly shaking hands with people, and, as a karate instructor in a style that emphasizes ground fighting and close up self defense, I roll around on the ground wrapped up in knots with people all the time, and yet, I rarely get sick, not even a sniffle. I haven't been to the doctor for anything more than an annual physical in years. On the rare occasion that I do catch a cold, I can always trace back about 10 days and find a prolonged occasion where my thoughts weren't where they needed to be – a time when I was in a funk about something.

REMARKABLE COURAGE

The Terror Barrier

So far it all sounds pretty easy, right? All you need to do to have the life of your dreams is just consciously think the right thoughts and hold that vision of what you want on the screen of your mind to the exclusion of all else. Okay! Got it! No problem! Pretty simple. Well, there's one other piece I need to make you aware of – because once you are aware of what happens, you will be able to combat it. Let's say you are doing everything right – you are imagineering your life as if you have already accomplished your goals; you're staying more positive; you're starting to believe. Then, one day, WHAM!!!!! - you find yourself scared to death. Fear, doubt, worry, anxiety creep in every time you start thinking about this new life that exists in your mind and is beginning to manifest in your reality. You hear a little voice inside your head saying, "You can't POSSIBLY earn that kind of revenue – do you really think you'll be able to break into that market – launch that new product? In this economy? Have you lost your mind? Why do you to think this time will be any different? You worked hard yesterday, why don't you just postpone that new client meeting and get a couple extra hours of sleep? You're a loser, you've always been a loser and you'll always be a loser!!" And on and on it goes. Well, my friend, you have just smacked head-long into what my mentor calls The Terror Barrier!!!!

First of all, CONGRATULATIONS!!! Jump up and down and celebrate these feelings and know that you are closer to your goal than you have ever been before!! The terror barrier is what happens when your goal, your vision, your WHY (whatever you want to call it) begins to seep into your subconscious mind. Remember, the subconscious mind is where all the old conditioning,

the paradigms, the habits and the self-image that have kept you stuck live. I affectionately call the old paradigms "Mr. X." Mr. X is very territorial and your new big goal that is seeping into your subconscious mind - let's call it "Mr. Y" is horning in on Mr. X's space. That voice that tells you that you can't do it is Mr. X - the fear, doubt and anxiety are his weapons to get you to run back to the safety and comfort of your old paradigm and kick Mr. Y (the new idea) out of your subconscious mind.

Don't give up! If you persist and keep going and crash through the terror barrier - keep visualizing your goal, continue to think about it and use your burning desire for it as fuel to continue in spite of the fear and the doubt - Mr. X will get weaker and weaker over time. The fear will diminish and the vision (Mr. Y) will get stronger. Then you know what happens? The "Y" idea becomes your new paradigm. How awesome is that!! You will end up with the self-image of a person with all the qualities of someone who effortlessly achieves the goal that you are pursuing!! And your "Y" conditioning will lead to "Y" actions and "Y" results until you reach your goal! What this also means is that you have to start over and build a new, even bigger vision because "Y" has now become your new "X." Do you follow me here? In life you're either creating or you're disintegrating – you can't stand still - you have to always be reaching for something beyond the here and now. That doesn't mean you can't be happy with where you are, but it does mean you should never be "satisfied"; you should always be striving for growth.

I'm sure if you think back you can identify example after example when you ran up against the Terror Barrier and acted in spite of the fear. Think about jumping off the high dive for the first time, your first dance or music recital, going on your first date, your first job interview, etc. Do you remember how terrified you were beforehand? Do you remember all the "what ifs" that cluttered your mind (what if it hurts...what if I make a fool of myself... what if I mess up... what if I don't know the answer...)? Think about one of those examples and then look at how you felt when it was over and you had acted in spite of the fear. Was it nearly as bad as you built it up in your mind to be? How did you feel after you accomplished it? Draw upon that experience to build your belief that you can do whatever you set out to do, no matter how scary it may be! Have the courage and the discipline to take action.

> During my time in the Virginia Tech Corps of Cadets, I had the opportunity to attend Army Airborne School. The purpose of the basic airborne course I attended was to "qualify the student in the use of the parachute as a means of combat deployment and to develop leadership, self-confidence, and an aggressive spirit through mental and physical conditioning." The course was three weeks long and consisted of three phases: "Ground Week", "Tower Week" and "Jump Week". Rigorous physical training (PT) was emphasized throughout the entire course.
>
> Ground week was stereotypical Army training – a lot like boot camp – very physically demanding, lots of inspections, lots of yelling. It was about learning technique at the basic level. I swear if I ever hear the term "PLF" (Parachute Landing Fall) again I will scream – I did hundreds of PLFs during that week and it seemed they were never right, never good enough.

Tower Week is about taking what you learned on the ground and adding height to the mix, all the while being yelled at and reminded that you don't know anything because you've never jumped before. By the time I got to Jump Week I couldn't wait to get up in the air and jump out of the darned plane. Even though I was excited and couldn't wait to get to the front of the line for my turn to jump, I cannot deny the moment of terror I felt when I was actually standing in the door of the plane looking out into empty space, but I jumped anyhow.

The funny thing is, it wasn't that big of a deal to make that first jump – it was fun! During Jump Week I had to make five jumps total. I was shocked at how loudly Mr. X started yammering in my ear as we prepared for the 2nd jump. I'd already done it once. I knew I could do it and that it was safe, but I was scared to death! I was not at all excited about getting to the front of the line this time. My palms were sweating, I was breathing hard, I was terribly anxious – even though I knew what was ahead of me. I kept hearing this voice in my head saying, "Are you sure you want to risk this? You've done it once, isn't that enough?" But, as I so often do, I told Mr. X to take a hike and jumped out of the plane anyhow. I proceeded to do that three more times and achieved my goal; I earned my jump wings!

Everyone has that little voice inside their head that talks to them every day. How many times do you hear that little voice during the day telling you what you can't do? This destructive internal dialogue has a sneaky way of infiltrating your attitude and setting up command. One of the questions I get all the time is: "How do I know if the voice in my head telling me I shouldn't act on my "Y" idea is Mr. X trying to keep me stuck or intuition moving me forward?" See, both Mr. X and intuition show up as that little voice in your head, so how do you know which is which? The answer is simple, if the voice is telling you to step back from your goal or your dream then Mr. X is the culprit, so do it anyway; jump out of the plane!

Purpose – The Fuel In The Engines

This brings me to the topic of Purpose. Remember back in Chapter 2, I contended that most people sleepwalk through life – never purposefully deciding where they want to go? The fact is that each and every person has a purpose in life, but, sadly, too many people either don't take the time to discover their true purpose in life or they spend their life trying to shove a square peg into a round hole - living their life in disharmony with their true calling (think about the man who dreams of and has a burning desire to become an actor but decides to become a lawyer and follow in the family practice because it is expected or because it is safe). A common trait you'll find among all successful and fulfilled people is that they are doing exactly what they want to do and living exactly as they wish to live.

I'd like to ask you to ponder the following questions for a moment: What would you attempt in life if you knew it was impossible to fail? Who would you want to be if you could make yourself over to be anyone? What would make you jump out of bed every morning excited about the day ahead? Does your current life reflect these answers? If it doesn't then you aren't living in alignment with your purpose. You have to ask yourself (and keep asking yourself), "What do I REALLY want?"

Think about the talents and gifts God has given you. We have been taught to base our decisions on what is logical and reasonable, ignoring the part of us that dreams; however, relying on logic forms the basis for rationalization and justification. Logic is based on your past experiences. Basing your decisions on logic is a sure-fire recipe for keeping you stuck right where you are because how on earth can you use past experience to get you somewhere you've never been?

For those of you who have found your purpose, I congratulate you; know that you're living the life of your dreams or are well on your way. Unfortunately, though, the majority of people are sleepwalking through life without direction. Purpose gives you direction, but determining your purpose in life is not a piece of cake either. I was fortunate. A quick analysis of my entire adult life revealed a common thread that was woven through all of my seemingly disjointed endeavors. In college I eagerly sought positions in the Corps of Cadets that offered me the opportunity to lead and train the underclassmen. Given my choice of assignments in the Air Force I chose to be an instructor pilot and then, an instructor of the instructors and then an evaluator of the instructors – even though there were a myriad of more glory-filled careers available to me in the military. In my green building consulting practice, I thrived on the opportunities to teach and present to other inspectors or to industry associations or realtors. As a black belt in Kempo Karate, I gained great joy and satisfaction in teaching others, especially the children. This common thread of teaching, coaching (I even coached at the high school varsity level for a time), and training defined my purpose in life, and, once I realized that and shifted my career to align with my purpose, the magic really started to happen.

Everyone is born with special gifts, talents and abilities as unique to them as their own fingerprint. Your gifts and talents are there for a reason; they allow you to live life to the fullest. If you've ever built a house, you know that you have to start with a schematic diagram. If you don't have a good blueprint, the end result may be something entirely different than you had hoped for. Your life is the same. You need a master plan, or purpose, upon which to build your life. If you listen to all of the high achievers, the self-help gurus, and the success coaches, you will find that they all agree on this point: defining your life's purpose is an essential part of achieving the goals you set for yourself.

Have you ever asked yourself, "Why am I here? What was I put on this earth to do?" I believe that determining your unique purpose gives meaning and hope to your life. Each one of us has something of incredible value to offer this world. You aren't meant to just exist on this planet. You were placed here for a reason and given the free will to find and fulfill it.

When you're in alignment with your purpose in life, the whole world tends to flow. Doors open automatically. People seem to appear on your path that can help you get what you want. You often seem to be in the right place at the right time. Life just seems to flow. Once you live "on purpose," you are open to life's possibilities and

opportunities. The more you live in alignment with your purpose, the less that life seems to be a struggle in other areas as well. What have you always dreamed about? Imagineer it, define it, and then go for it!

Every day, you exchange your life for what you do. If you lose items or money, you can get them back, but you can never retrieve time. So make sure you spend your life the way that is right for you. Is that job you hate worth your life? How about the financial struggles? The bad relationship? Is it worth your life? Understanding your life's purpose allows you to focus on what is most important to you and where you will have the biggest impact on other people's lives. A highly talented artist can certainly choose to be a doctor, but if their true calling is to be a painter, then you certainly wouldn't want them to operate on you, would you?

Finding and living your purpose gives you an understanding of who you are, and it will impact your thoughts, choices, feelings, and actions. The equation holds: if your thoughts, feelings and actions are in true alignment with your purpose, then you will create results in harmony with who you are at your core. Some of you may feel a bit "stuck," and I often hear adults jokingly say, "I don't know what I want to be when I grow up." I absolutely know that feeling – there were so many years that I floundered – something was missing. I knew that there was more to life than what I was doing. I didn't feel fulfilled, but didn't really know what I wanted.

Your purpose in life is not something you decide with your intellect; you discover it. You will know when you have discovered it because it feels right and it fills you with energy. This might seem like a difficult concept, and that is okay. Your purpose has its origin in your values, talents and abilities. It is the essence of who you are; it is everything that is meaningful to you. Your values and highest held beliefs will come into alignment as you become the expression of your true self, your true core. Everyone has special talents and the ability to create fantastic things in their lives as well. Whether it is in the area you are currently working or in a totally different area, your special talents exist. You just have to find them and have the courage to take action.

The fact is when you are living on purpose it makes it easier to find the courage to act in spite of fear. The fear is going to be there regardless – there is not much you can do about that, but when you are on purpose and you have a burning desire to achieve that purpose, it makes it so much easier to tell Mr. X to get out of town.

TOOL: THE 3-3-3 CONCEPT

In the book *You Were Born Rich*, the author relates a story about Bob Templeton, a man who was an executive in a telecommunications company that owned radio stations across Canada. He had witnessed the aftermath of a devastating tornado in the town of Barrie, Ontario, and he wanted to do something to help the people in the town. He decided that he was going to figure out a way to raise a large sum of money immediately to give to the town of Barrie.

The next week he called all of the top executives in the company into a meeting and asked them if they wanted to raise $3 million, three days hence in only three hours, and give the money to the town. The people in the meeting began spitting out all the reasons why this was an insane idea, but Templeton stopped them saying, "I didn't ask you if we could, or even if we should, I asked you if you would like to." Of course, everyone's charitable nature wanted to help the town, so Templeton took a page of a large flip chart and drew a big "T" on the page. On the left side of the T he wrote "Why We Can't" and on the right side of the T he wrote "How We Can." Then, on the "Why We Can't" side of the chart he drew a big "X" that encompassed the whole column.

Templeton was aware of both the Law of Polarity—for every up there's a down, for every good there's a bad, and for every reason why we can't there is a reason why we CAN—and the power of perception. So, he told the people in the meeting that there was no room to write down any reasons why they couldn't raise the money in the specified time—regardless of how valid the reasons might be—and, if someone brought up a reason why it couldn't be done, the rest of the room was to say "NEXT" until a positive idea came up. By concentrating on how they could achieve their objective, the Telemedia Company did indeed raise over $3 million during a 3 hour trans-Canada radio-thon, which occurred 3 days after that fateful meeting.

The power of this decision making and brainstorming tool comes in focusing 100% of your attention on how you CAN accomplish something – even if the method of accomplishing it seems completely outlandish. You are not allowed to spend any energy on why you can't accomplish whatever it is you are pondering. We use this method in our business all the time and it is truly amazing how we have moved from what seemed to be a completely unworkable, blocked situation to a solution (usually in the most improbable way) over and over again. By using this concept, you can have whatever you want! Put your focus on HOW YOU CAN – even in the smallest way, and "NEXT" every idea telling you why you can't. It is a difficult exercise in the beginning, but you will find that positive ideas will start racing into your mind! Remember, you don't have to know the whole plan. Just make the decision and the steps will become apparent to you as you go along.

8 | FLIGHT PLANNING SECRETS

"If you fail to plan then you are planning to fail." This quote is attributed to Benjamin Franklin, and I absolutely agree with this philosophy on so many levels! You must have a plan if your want to achieve success!! At this point, you may be saying, "Now wait a second! Throughout this book you have been saying that I just need to hold my goal on the screen of my mind and feel like it has already manifested. You say that I shouldn't know the 'How!'" Yes, when I am speaking of your ultimate goal, that is very true – you shouldn't try to plan your way to your goal because, if you have the right goal, you won't have any clue how you're going to get there! However, when you're figuring out what you need to do to get from today to next week, you absolutely need a plan – you need to know what your schedule is and when your meetings are and what your obligations are and so on. It provides a certain level of accountability when you know what you are expected to do each day.

~~Time~~ Activity Management

One area that many people struggle with in terms of planning is "time" management. This is actually a misnomer – there is no way to manage time. The most productive corporate executive gets the same amount of time each day as the hobo on the bench – you get all there is, 24 hours each day. It's not managing time that is the problem, rather managing the activities that fill that time. Those individuals who are able to effectively manage their activities (rather than rely on crisis management) tend to be the highest achievers in all walks of life—from business to sports to public service. If you can learn to manage your day-to-day activities well, then you will be able to function effectively, even under intense pressure. I hate to burst your bubble, but the more successful you become, the longer your to-do list will get. The point is that as you get better at managing your activities, it will seem that you accelerate through your day and get an incredible amount accomplished.

In order to shift your mindset regarding time so you will work smarter and improve time utilization, you must concentrate on results, not on being busy. Activity management is not rocket science. It typically does not require intense thinking or research to understand. What is much more important is how much those activity management principles and techniques are integrated into your daily routine—how habitual they become, so they penetrate into your subconscious mind. This is why learning in small bits over an extended period of time, with each of those bits repeated over and over again (spaced repetition), will beat the effect of any intense "time management" seminar.

Do you put off important tasks repeatedly? If your answer is yes, you're not alone. In fact, procrastination afflicts the vast majority of people in one way or another. Unfortunately, for some, procrastination has become such a bad habit that it prevents them from doing even the smallest of tasks and disrupts their life. Procrastinators work as many hours per day as other people (and often work longer hours), but they invest their time in the wrong activities.

Some procrastinate because they simply don't understand how to prioritize. For others, procrastination is a reaction to a feeling of being overwhelmed. For many people, it stems from not believing they're capable of completing a task; as a result, they work on what is easiest, leaving the more difficult items for "another day." Unfortunately, the big task isn't going to go away and other items will inevitably be added so the list just keeps getting longer and longer. Worse still are those who do not act because they are afraid of failure. Others just aren't organized enough to figure out what they need to do to complete a task. There are many causes of procrastination, but, where the rubber meets the road, there is really one main reason for it—you just don't want to do a certain activity.

Procrastination costs us a great deal in terms of time and money, both personally and professionally. All procrastinators must learn that there is never a perfect time to start a job. Just do it and don't stop until you're finished. The bottom line is that it takes courage to make decisions and to act – it takes bold moves and guts to reach for your goals, but, if there is no action, there can be no results. No guts, no glory!

There is an interesting maxim called Parkinson's Law (attributed to Cyril Northcote Parkinson) that states, "Work expands so as to fill the time available for its completion." Have you ever noticed how that works for most people? In school the teacher gives you an assignment and tells you it is due a week from Tuesday. Despite your best intentions to work on it a little bit each day, what happens? Yep, Monday night you find yourself pulling an all-nighter to complete the assignment just under the wire. The pattern tends to play out for most people into their careers as well – putting off work until just before the boss' deadline. It is a very interesting phenomenon. Now, don't hate me, but I can say with all honesty that I have never been a procrastinator. I was conditioned very early on to decide and act and that's just the way I have lived my life. It's a matter of discipline; it's a matter of accountability; however, I've seen procrastination weave its insidious spell on the people around me all my life and there is a common theme among all of the procrastinators I have known – they were all nearly phobic about making decisions. Isn't that interesting? (More on that in the next chapter.)

The key to controlling and, ultimately, combating this destructive habit is to make a conscious effort to recognize when you start procrastinating, figure out why it happens, and then decide to take proactive steps to eliminate it from your life. If you're putting off starting a project because you find it overwhelming, try to break the project into a set of smaller, more manageable tasks. Once you accomplish one small task, you'll start to feel that you're achieving things, and, soon, the whole project will seem very achievable.

Take writing this book, for example. The idea of writing a whole book is a daunting task, taken as a whole, and the deadline given for its completion was ridiculously short (three weeks). There was no room to procrastinate even if I had wanted to – in fact, the whole notion seemed positively impossible; however, once I broke the book down into an outline and then determined how many pages I needed to write each day, I was able to work on each section of each chapter individually, focusing my effort and attention on each piece as a standalone action item. The process flowed much better and more quickly than I ever thought possible – I even finished the manuscript ahead of schedule!

Regardless of your reason for procrastinating, you must break this destructive habit if you are ever to succeed. This nasty habit will cause you to miss opportunities and could even derail your career or your life. If you're completely honest with yourself, you probably know when you're procrastinating. Have the discipline and the courage to stick to your priorities.

When I first started my business, I felt I needed to be accessible to my clients all the time, but it became apparent that I was spending hours every day in crisis management mode—putting out fires. I found out that I am much more effective and efficient in my role if I unplug from the outside world at times and focus on those tasks that allow me to reach the maximum number of people—writing this book, for instance, or planning and preparing seminars. Remember, there is an important distinction between procrastination and exercising good activity management. It may be better to delay an unimportant task in order to focus on something of a higher priority. Think about your career. What is the purpose of your job versus what you spend the bulk of your time doing? Think about how much more effective you could be in your job if you concentrated on the tasks that were consistent with the true purpose of your position.

This is also true in most people's personal lives. Think about that yard long "to do" list that you have at home. What if you started devoting just a couple of hours every weekend to one task on that list—think how much you would accomplish over the course of a month or a year.

Understand the reasons for procrastination and find ways to motivate yourself to get moving every single day. Daily action toward your goal is such a huge key to your success. I discussed the concept of inertia earlier – when you are moving you tend to keep moving, but once you stop it's hard to get going again. As an author I was dumbfounded when an incredibly prolific author suggested that I write just one page per day. He said that if I would do that I would have a 365 page book in one year – that's a decent sized book! Such a simple, but powerful concept – a short-term plan backed by consistent, daily action toward your goal!

Tool: Daily Commitment Sheet

Almost 100 years ago a management consultant named Ivy Lee was doing some work with Charles Schwab, the head of Bethlehem Steel at the time. Schwab was lamenting that his biggest obstacle to true, runaway success in the steel business was in the effectiveness of his management team – they just didn't do a very good job of utilizing their time.

Lee told Schwab that in 20 minutes he could show him a technique that would multiply the effectiveness and productivity of himself and his entire team. Schwab asked him how much it would cost and Lee said that was up to him - to try it for a few weeks and then to send him a check for whatever he thought it was worth. Schwab gave Lee the go-ahead to spend 20 minutes with each member of his team to introduce his system. A few weeks later, Schwab sent Lee a check for $25,000 (that's equivalent to ~$500,000 today) as compensation for the tool he had provided them with.

Here is Lee's system as it was given to the executives at Bethlehem Steel in the 1920's: Each evening before leaving your office take a blank Commitment Sheet and write down, in order of priority, the top six things you will do the following day that will help you move toward your goal. They should be achievable during the following day. Clear your desk of all extraneous papers except for your Daily Commitment Sheet and leave the office.

The next morning when you come to the office take your list and start with #1 on the list. Give no thought to #2, just give your full focus and attention to #1. When #1 is complete, move to #2 on the list. Give no thought to #1 and do not anticipate #3, just focus on #2 until it is complete. Then move to #3... Work through the list in this manner until your list is complete. Before you leave the office at the end of the day, complete a commitment sheet for the next day.

Now, this process works great if your goal IS in complete alignment with your full time job, but, what if you have a goal that has nothing to do with what you do for a living? For example, let's assume that you have a goal of starting your own business and earning $1,000,000 per year in personal income, but, at the moment, you are working a 9am - 5pm job that is meeting your needs while you pursue your dream. How do you apply Lee's system in that case? It is important to understand that your Daily Commitment Sheet is NOT a day-planner – it is not your schedule. It is to be completed with the constraints of the next day's schedule in mind. Let's look at an example. Say, your day planner for tomorrow looks something like this:

7:00	Take child to the bus stop
9:30	Staff Meeting
11:00	Sales Presentation
12:30	Lunch with Bill Smith (XYZ Corp)

2:00	Admin Time in Office
4:00	Sales Presentation
5:30	Pick up child from After-School Care
7:00	Family Dinner

On the face, there doesn't seem to be a lot of free time for "goal achieving" activities, does there? But remember, I'm not talking about leaping from the starting point to the manifestation of your big, beautiful dream in one day – not at all! This is about choosing six things – no matter how small – that will advance you a fraction of a baby step toward your ultimate goal. Now, that said, you don't put items on the list that you do habitually – you wouldn't put "Brush teeth" on your commitment sheet because that's a habit and you would do it anyway. You don't want to put mundane tasks on the list either like "Go to the grocery store" – that's not advancing you toward your goal, unless perhaps you're going to the grocery store to buy food for a cocktail party you are hosting for potential investors in your new business – do you see the difference?

So, given the schedule constraints for the day, the items that go on the Commitment Sheet might be:

1. Review sba.gov website and locate Grants section
2. Call John Smith at ABC Bank to discuss business checking account options
3. Call Jane Doe (prospective investor) and schedule lunch

4. Drop by Chamber of Commerce and pick up membership application
5. Call Jack (your attorney) and schedule golf on Saturday to discuss LLC vs. Corporation
6. Read article on "The New Entrepreneurial Edge" in Inc. magazine.

None of these items are incredibly time consuming, but they are still prioritized. You can check out the website between taking Junior to the bus stop and heading to the office. The calls and stop at the Chamber could be made en route to your other appointments during the day. And the article could be read before you go to bed. Each of the tasks are action oriented and move you a little closer to your goal. When you are prioritizing your tasks for the next day, push yourself even harder and choose the task that makes you most uncomfortable and make that the #1 thing you will do! Make a habit of attacking the thing that you least want to do first – it will not only get it out of the way up front (helping to keep your vibration high), but it will also kill that nasty tendency to procrastinate!!

We talk a lot about focusing on the ultimate goal, and you absolutely should be doing so as often as possible throughout the day; however, when you are completing your Daily Commitment Sheet, your six commitments should be absolutely logical and planned – you can see the next step and you know what you need to do to complete it. If you look at your goal on a graph, it looks something like this:

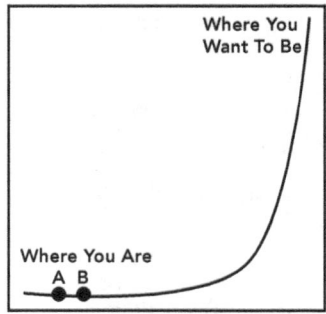

You have no idea how you are going to get from where you are right now to where you want to ultimately be – it is exponential growth; it is illogical, but look at points A and B – they're right beside each other – B is only very slightly higher than A – you can logically SEE and PLAN how to move from point A to point B. That's what I'm talking about with your daily commitments – planned, achievable, action oriented tasks that move you along the curve from day to day. That being said, it is CRITICAL that you always have your ultimate vision – your GOAL - in mind. Without it, you will "logic yourself to death." You will work on these six tasks each day that are planned and very linear, but you will never follow the curve upwards toward your goal. You'll just keep plodding along, day after day, on what seems like a straight line, but, in fact, since nothing can stand still - you are either creating or disintegrating - if you are not following the curve up to your goal, you are actually going backwards – disintegrating. To illustrate the point graphically, your progress actually looks like this:

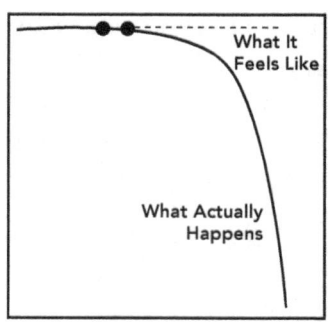

You have to keep upping the ante, so to speak, and the only way to make sure that you are tackling the tasks that will move you along that upward curve to your goal is to constantly have that vision in your mind and keep asking yourself: "Will this action (this task or commitment) take me closer to my goal?" If the answer is "Yes," then great - do it; however, if the answer is "No," pick another task for your Daily Commitment Sheet.

One last point about the items you choose for your Daily Commitment Sheet. We've mentioned that the tasks need to be achievable within the day. PLEASE do not use your Daily Commitment Sheet as a "stick!" In other words, don't get wrapped up in the idea that you need to put items on your list to FORCE yourself to do them. Force negates everything, and, if you are putting things on your list that would be better served by waiting for a day when you have a large block of time to devote to them, please wait! For example, if your goal was to launch a new business six months from now and your day planner for tomorrow looked like the one a few pages back, you wouldn't want to list "Write a business plan" as one of your six items – there's just not enough time in the day to accomplish it – unless you want to pull an all-nighter - but you might list "Look up Business Plan templates online" on your list – that could easily be done in 30 minutes or less. Save your business plan creation for a day when your schedule is less cramped. It is critically important that your list be achievable. I am not suggesting you procrastinate; I am simply begging you to not use your commitment sheet as a means of forcing square pegs into round holes.

Let's discuss for a moment the habits that using this sheet will foster.

1. **Prioritization:** Knowing not only what you need to do, but also what is most important is an essential goal achieving quality.
2. **Productivity and Effectiveness:** Ending each day by completing your Daily Commitment Sheet allows

your subconscious mind to see what's coming for the next day and, at the same time, be focused on your goal. Your subconscious mind will literally work on the various tasks all night long while you sleep. You will find that you will wake up with intuitive bursts that will help you move toward your goal – and get your list accomplished!

3. **Success:** When you have the experience of having all six items on your Daily Commitment Sheet checked off day after day, you build a success mindset (rather than working from that ponderous "To Do" list that all of us have that never seems to get any shorter and makes you feel like you're constantly spinning your wheels). Regardless of what else happened that day, you completed the six most important things that will move you toward your goal – the day was a success. Success breeds success. One day will build on the next and before you know it you will find that your goal has manifested!

4. **Keeping Commitments:** Most people fall into one of two camps when it comes to making and keeping their commitments. They are either not very good at keeping commitments to anyone OR they ARE good at keeping the commitments they make to other people, but they ARE NOT very good at keeping the commitments they make to themselves. By completing your Daily Commitment Sheet and checking off each item every day, you are building the habit of making and KEEPING commitments to yourself. This is so huge!! Just imagine what your life would be if every time you said "I should..." you actually DID!!

In summary, here's how you use your Daily Commitment Sheet (download a Template and instructions for its use at DebCheslow.com/dailycommitment):

- **Before going to bed each day make a prioritized list of the six things you need to do the following day to move you toward your goal within the constraints of your schedule;**
- **The next day, as pockets of time are available begin working on task #1 with your full focus until it is complete;**
- **Then move on to task #2 – no attention to #1, no anticipation of #3;**
- **Proceed through your list until all six items are complete;**
- **Congratulate yourself on a job well done; and**
- **Make a list for the next day.**

I use the Daily Commitment Sheet in my work life, as well as my personal life, and it has made a tremendous difference. You see, you can apply the knowledge that you have received about your mind to any area of your life where you would like to improve your results – whether it's your income, your relationships, your weight, your spirituality – ANYTHING!! It all works together.

DEB CHESLOW

MY DAILY COMMITMENTS

I, _____, commit to complete the following five tasks that will move me closer to my goals by the end of today, _____, 20____

Number One

☐ COMPLETE

Number Two

☐ COMPLETE

Number Three

☐ COMPLETE

Number Four

☐ COMPLETE

Number Five

☐ COMPLETE

Number Six

☐ COMPLETE

"Every action we take, everything we do is either a victory or defeat in the struggle to become what we want to be."
~Ninon de L'Enclos

Your signature is a symbol of the commitment you have made to yourself for today. In learning to keep our commitments, not only to others, but also to ourselves, we find the journey to the attainment of our goals is a much smoother, straighter line.

Compliments of The Simple Success Solutions
www.thesimplesuccesssolutions.com
(386) 308-2155

_____
SIGNATURE

9 | AIM, <u>FIRE</u>, READY

Let's talk for a little bit about decision making. Are you good at making decisions? Most people aren't; in fact, if you are like 97% of people out there you probably HATE making decisions and were never really taught HOW to make them. When approaching a decision, most people follow the old adage, "Ready, Aim, Fire." The problem is they never get past the "Ready" phase. They get a great idea and then get stuck in get ready to get ready mode, never getting around to pulling the trigger and making the decision to take action. Effective people reorder the equation: "Aim, Fire, Ready." They get the great idea, then they make the decision and move into action, and only THEN do they worry about figuring out "how" they are going to make it all happen.

Decision making is certainly not taught in school, yet it is without a doubt the most important skill a person can have when it comes to improving their life. If you think about it, most people are very indecisive – either they put off making decisions or they just ask other people for THEIR opinion on the matter and then make a decision based upon the collective input they receive. That is no way to go through life.

Decision and Circumstances

The power of a decision and the ability to make decisions will propel your life forward in ways you can't even imagine! How often have you caught yourself saying, "I would like to do (or have, or be) "X," but I can't because…?" Whatever follows "because" is a circumstance. You can allow your current circumstances to limit your life or you can completely disregard them in relation to your decision making processes.

The biggest circumstantial stumbling blocks for most people are TIME and MONEY. I refuse to let time or money enter into my decision making process. Now most people say, "Oh sure, nice for you, Deb; you don't have to consider money because you already have plenty of it and you own your own company so if you want to take time to do something, you can." Let me assure that wasn't always the case! There were times during my journey when I wasn't exactly sure how we were going to sustain ourselves for the next month or how on earth I was ever going to complete the 85 items on my "to do" list that HAD to be done in a given week, but, once I made the decision to forge ahead anyhow – even though I didn't have the time or the money and had no idea where it was going to come from, what I needed always came!!!

Once you make a committed decision, time and money just tend to show up! Now, I'm not talking about money falling out of the sky (although sometimes that happens – I'll go out to the mailbox and there's an unexpected check), and I'm *certainly* not talking about going out and racking up a bunch of credit card debt. I am talking about having the courage to make a decision to do something and then take action on that decision. Remember, courage is not the absence of fear; it is taking action in spite of that fear. I can assure you that once you make the decision, your behavior will change to make room in your schedule and your budget. Whether your current financial circumstances allow you to afford something or not should not be a consideration—the only thing you need to take into account is a) do you want it? and b) will it move you closer to your goal? Then make a decision right then, right where you are, with what you have.

> *I have two teenage daughters—they were both born in Colorado, but we moved away when they were too young to remember anything about it. Ever since they were small children, they asked me to take them to see Colorado. I kept putting off the trip because either the money for such an extensive trip or the time away from work always seemed elusive. As my older daughter was nearing the end of high school, I got fed up and just decided to make the reservations for the trip. No surprise, I found the time and money without much effort. Think about your own life and I'm sure you can relate. Most people would never take a vacation if they waited for the time and the money to be there before deciding to go.*

Circumstances should never be the determining factor in the decision making process because circumstances are only temporary. Refuse to allow your current constraints (money, people, time, etc.) to enter into the equation. When you are faced with a decision you need to view it as if you were brand new to planet Earth and

had Aladdin's lamp in your hands and could create any reality you wished. Too many people use their current circumstances as a crutch—a reason why they can't make a decision or a reason why they "can't," period. They use their current circumstances as the fall guy for why they decide not to go for whatever it is that they want.

I find it very interesting that the people I see who allow their circumstances to dictate their actions are the very same people who walk around blaming others for their situation, complaining about their circumstances and justifying why they won't take action at all. Let me be very clear here: You will NEVER be successful – truly successful – until you take full responsibility for that success. YOU have to be the one to own your situation because, like it or not, you created it. If you don't like where you are in your life or you don't like the results you are experiencing in your business, you absolutely have the power to change, but you have to take full responsibility for that change – no one is going to do it for you!

When I started my consulting business I was a one-woman show, and I did everything from sales to bookkeeping to delivery myself. Things were going great! I was focused on sales, so sales manifested each and every day. Then one day, I got the idea that I should recruit a sales force to handle sales. I took my eye off the ball and waited for this grand sales force to go out and "do it for me." I stopped selling. It was an experiment that failed miserably! Once I resumed responsibility for my company's sales, revenue picked up again and the company has been very successful ever since. Now, that doesn't mean your company can't have a sales force, it just means that you can't surrender the responsibility for sales and revenue and *hope* that the sales force will make huge things happen for you.

Another important point I want to make here is that making a decision and then falling short is not a failure! It is only a failure when you decide to quit. "Falling short" creates opportunities for growth, which actually will propel you forward in the direction of your goals. Remember, the only time you really FAIL is when you give up and quit.

The point is you must have the courage to actually make decisions. Every successful person I have ever encountered makes solid decisions and follows through on those decisions with massive action. They do not second guess their decisions, and they are bold in taking action.

One of my very favorite stories about the power of decision goes back to the early 1960's when President John F. Kennedy asked Dr. Werner von Braun, Director of the Marshall Flight Center at Redstone Arsenal, what it would take to build a rocket that would carry a man to the moon and return him safely to earth. Von Braun could have responded with a HUGE laundry list of obstacles that the generation's present circumstances presented, but rather he replied with five simple words, "The will to do it!" The technology to achieve such a task did not exist (other than in someone's imagination), it would cost HUGE sums of money and time that weren't currently available, and the danger was great, but those were not considerations in the decision to do it—those were only the present circumstances. President Kennedy made the decision, announced it, and, by the end of the decade, the United States celebrated as Neil Armstrong took "one small step for man, one giant leap for mankind" and stepped out of the Apollo 11 capsule onto the surface of the moon and returned safely to Earth with his crew only days later.

Everything is a Decision

No matter how you look at it, the truth is that decisions are responsible for the results you get in your life. See, even when you don't make a decision, you have in reality made a decision to not make a decision. Some people, lacking confidence, always want others to decide for them, and, as a result, they end up living according to someone else's wishes. Something as hugely important as the skill of effective decision making should be taught in school, but it's not and, until recently, corporations hadn't integrated it into their training programs either.

Armed with the proper information, and, by subjecting yourself to certain disciplines, you can become a very effective decision maker.

In my private consulting practice, in my speaking business and in my books, I really focus on the skill of disciplined, effective decision making. Unfortunately, most people let logic drive the decision making process. Most people are taught from a very early age to look at the pros and cons, analyze the situation carefully, look at all of the "what ifs," but what you need to understand is that your logic is driven by your paradigms, by your experience, and by your past. As a result, your logic (Mr. X) is guaranteed to keep you stuck right where you are, living like you've always lived, acting like you've always acted, living in the past—if you rely on it alone. You must learn to acknowledge logic and take what is relevant but not to let it control you. To grow and live and prosper you must be willing to be illogical.

Think about it for a second, was it logical for Edison to doggedly pursue the path to the incandescent light – especially when he failed thousands of times? Was it logical for the Wright Brothers to believe that they could get something heavier than air to soar above the ground? Was it logical for me to accept a general scholarship in college (that would secure my career as an Air Force engineer) as a path to become an Air Force Instructor Pilot? Was it logical for me to start my business in the middle of the worst recession of my time? NO! There's nothing logical about any of those scenarios, but all of these situations involved people with a burning desire to achieve something completely illogical and a belief that they would succeed despite the long odds against them. That takes courage – courage to spit in the face of logic and step into action in ways that most people would deem ridiculous.

Making decisions is a simple process. It's something we should teach our children when they are young. It's as simple as answering a question. Think about the discussion about perception—for every good there is a bad, for every up, a down; well, for every question there is an answer.

Other people's opinions of you don't matter. Yours is the only one that is important. Those who have become very proficient at making decisions, without being influenced by the opinions of others, are the same people who appear to "have it all" to the outside world. Their entire lives are dominated by the power of sound decision making.

> *Studying karate has been a life long dream for me – something I had wanted to do since I was 8 years old - but I didn't actually start training until I was 38 years old and decided the time was now! The decision was completely illogical. On the surface, I was too old to start training in earnest; I didn't have the time as a single parent*

of two young girls; I didn't have the money for the classes and all the equipment and such; but I started classes in spite of the odds against my success. Four years later, I earned my black belt (and later 1st, 2nd and 3rd degree black belts) and became an instructor. My decision to begin studying karate ultimately helped me find my purpose in life—to teach and train others to reach down deep inside themselves and find the courage to reach beyond what they believe to be possible and achieve their potential. The key is that my decision was a committed decision, and, although I encountered many obstacles and the path was a long and difficult one and I should have quit at many different junctions, I stuck with it, come what may.

When you make a decision, commit to it and don't give up. You want to make decisions quickly and efficiently; learning to decide right here, right now with what you've got (that doesn't mean being reckless; it just means not letting logic forestall the decision forever). Decision making is a crucial part of all of our lives.

Every time one of my clients talks about an unfulfilled dream, I ask them why they haven't taken action. I hear all sorts of excuses: "I don't have the money," "I don't have time" or "My kids are too little." These are all smokescreens which cover up the real reason. I explain to them that they don't need the time or the money until they actually make the decision to do, have or be the thing that they will need the money or time for. Then, once the decision is made,

they will figure out a way to make their dream come true. The real reason people have unfulfilled lives is because of a lack of decision making. Until you make the decision to take action, nothing happens. On the other hand, once you make a committed decision you will always attract what you need to make that decision a reality.

> Last summer, Angie and I were looking for a fitness challenge. We were bored with the same old workout routines and were looking for something new to train for. Angie discovered that there was a 120 mile Gran Fondo Bike Race in Daytona Beach (very near our home) right before Thanksgiving that year, so – even though neither of us knew anything about bike racing, endurance cycling, training for an endurance event, bicycle maintentance or nutrition for endurance events, not to mention the fact that we didn't even OWN road bikes - we decided to register and train for the event. In truth, ANGIE decided to register us and then broadcast our intention to the world over social media before we could change our minds – now that's accountability! We were committed – the decision was made. We went to the bike shop and found two very nice Trek road bikes and picked out all the necessary accessories and such. We found a training program that would get us ready for the race in 10 weeks. We hired a personal trainer to dial in our physical training for an endurance event. Then, we saw what we were in for and sheer panic set in. Our training

program had us on the bikes four days per week for HOURS! The weekly endurance ride started at 30 miles and then ramped up in distance every week from there. There were interval rides and strength rides and recovery rides and twice weekly training sessions – where on earth were we going to find the time to fit all of this extra training into an already jam-packed work and family schedule? How could we possibly justify it?

Angie then pointed out that it WAS our business to be physcially fit. As the authors of a book that prescribed a healthy lifestyle, Release – The Simple Success Solution for Real and Permanent Weight Loss, and the creators of a corporate wellness program, it was our job to be a "product of our product" and to inspire others to achieve things that are beyond reasonable. Once we changed our perception to view the training for the bike race as an integral part of our business (as opposed to a frivolous luxury), it was quite easy to fit it into our days. Not only did we fit hours of extra training each week into a schedule that was incredibly busy already, but we also accomplished several other huge, unrealistic projects during the same period of time. The circumstance of "no time" was simply a matter of perception, and, once our perception shifted from luxury to responsibility, the time was available.

When you are confronted with a personal decision, do you struggle painfully, procrastinate, and finally ask someone else to decide for you? Does it get harder when you are dealing with a decision with long-term consequences such as a making a major purchase, selecting a home or a career, or deciding whether or not to get married? Worse still, even after the decision is made, do you keep wondering if a different choice would have been better? If your answer to these questions is "yes," then, like most people from all walks of life, you are likely not living life to its fullest. Decision making doesn't have to be difficult.

Indecision causes disintegration – you are either creating or disintegrating, nothing stands still. You are either moving forward or you are going backwards – status quo is a myth- it doesn't exist. The most effective people out there are those who make decisions right where they are with the information they have in the moment. They commit to their decision and are unlikely to change their mind without great deliberation.

If you study people who are really good at making decisions, you'll find that they all possess another wonderful quality – self-confidence. They believe they can do, have or be anything they set their minds to – failure doesn't really enter into the equation. If things don't work out the way they planned, they shrug it off quickly and keep moving forward; they view it as a lesson, not a failure. So, let me ask you a question… Are you hoping that the concepts in this book will work for you or have you **decided** that they will? There's a tremendous difference. Hoping leads to guaranteed failure, while a committed decision leads to guaranteed success. Again, what would your life be like if every time you said, "I should…," you actually DID?

Advance Decision Making

When planning a trip, what is the first thing you do? You make reservations with the airline, the hotel, the rental car company, etc., so that you can get to your destination hassle free and have your accommodations waiting for you, right? I don't know about you, but I would find it incredibly stressful to wake up on the day of a trip, knowing that I needed to be in San Diego by dinner time and just HOPE that I could get a seat on a plane and have a place to sleep in San Diego when I got there. No, you don't do that. You make decisions about your journey before you ever take the first step on the trip.

You also don't buy your ticket to San Diego and then get to the airport and see all the other nifty destinations that you could go to and throw your ticket in the trash and go to Omaha instead, even though your hotel, your rental car, your family, friends and the convention you need to attend are all in San Diego!! Why shouldn't you employ this same technique – advance decision making - when it comes to your journey to your goal? Think about it, if you DECIDE that, come what may, you will do certain things without fail, then it doesn't matter that you get a call from your buddy suggesting that you ditch work after lunch and watch the big game – you've already made your decision. Making decisions in advance can solve so many problems and take the guesswork or surprise out of things! You are holding your ticket to your dream life in your hands – don't just throw it in the trash when something seemingly more attractive, but unrelated to your dream, comes along.

Deciding NOT To Decide

In the last chapter I commented on the fact that all the people I know who have an issue with procrastination appear to have one trait in common – they have difficulty making decisions. Maybe it's bearing responsibility for their decisions that is the problem, or maybe it's the commitment to doing what the decision requires that trips them up. Regardless of their reason, the root cause lies in their self image. So take heart! If procrastination is a problem in your life, you have all the tools you need right here in this book to tweak your self-image and banish this dream stealer from your life!

Tool: The 4 Questions

Anytime you need to make a decision, there are four questions you need to ask yourself:

1. Do I want to be, to do or to have this?
2. Will being, doing or having this move me in the direction of my goals?
3. Is being, doing or having this in harmony with God's laws or the laws of the universe?
4. Will being, doing or having this violate the rights of others?

If you answer "Yes" to questions 1-3 and "No" to question 4, then you make your decision right where you are with what you have and move forward!

It takes courage to make decisions. Decision makers are leaders. Leadership is all about making decisions, and, if you are to last in that position, you had better learn to make the right ones. People will not respect or follow a leader for very long if they cannot make the right decisions. When faced with a decision, don't allow yourself to procrastinate – stand up to the disintegrative power of indecision; ask yourself The 4 questions and then make your decision – right where you are with what you've got!

10 | FLY – FIGHT - WIN

In the preceding chapters, I have shared a systemized strategy for success; a system that I learned in the Air Force teaching airmen to fly advanced supersonic jets; a system the Air Force has used since its inception to create phenomenal results. It is a system based upon the four foundational pillars of discipline, accountability, standards and systems, and the beautiful part is that it is a system that can be duplicated by any individual, team, company or organization to finally get the results they want. It works every time for the people who take it to heart and apply it every single day, but despite the best of intentions, there are times when life throws you a curveball – something you never saw coming – and you have to adjust, pivot and respond quickly. It's like being up in a jet and having an engine flame out – there's no time for "Woe is me" – it's adjust and compensate and fix the problem on the spot or crash. This chapter provides guidance for handling these unforeseen circumstances, so that, at the end of the day, you have a smooth landing.

Weld The Escape Hatches Closed

Success is based on taking risks. Remaining in your comfort zone won't move you forward – the magic happens outside your comfort zone! When you make the decision to pursue a goal, obstacles will inevitably pop up along the way. You have to be ready and willing to face those obstacles head-on and deal with any problems that ensue. You cannot allow your fear of failure to prevent you from reaching your goals and desires.

Somewhere along the way, people started being conditioned with a failure avoidance mentality. So many people are absolutely paralyzed by fear when it comes to making decisions and taking risk because they are so scared they will fail. What if history's great inventors had felt that way? We'd still be reading by candlelight, writing with a quill and ink and riding a horse to work! People seem to feel that they have to have a "Plan B" – a fallback position so that, if things don't work out, everything will be okay. I don't buy that! I believe that if you have a Plan B in place then Plan B is your REAL plan.

I find it absolutely amazing how many people I talk to that focus on failure. They get this great big idea and then they "what if I fail" themselves to death. If you haven't figured it out yet, let me make it super clear for you - YOU GET WHAT YOU FOCUS ON. When you focus on failure (or the possibility of failure), you are planning on it. When you believe that you will be successful in an endeavor – whatever it might be - and completely ignore the possibility of failure then you will succeed. I call it welding the escape hatches closed.

You see, if you are going after something big you will inevitably run up against the Terror Barrier – you can't help it. Fear, doubt and worry are going to creep into your mind just as surely as the sun will rise tomorrow morning. If you have an escape hatch, a safety net, call it what you will – you will take it. If you weld the escape hatches closed, you have no choice but to press on. If you give yourself a back-up plan, that becomes THE plan. You know what I'm talking about, right? "If my business goes under, I can always get a job..." "If I don't like college, I can always go home..." "If my marriage doesn't work out, then I can always get a divorce..." Your thoughts become things!!!!

Welding the escape hatches closed takes courage – there's no doubt about that. It is incredibly uncomfortable to embark on a journey that has a high degree of risk involved. If people didn't have the guts to take risks, would people ever start new businesses? Would they launch new products? Invest in research and development? Have children? NO! You can't eliminate risk – anything worth having involves risk; without risk there can be no reward. Have the courage to step boldly in the direction of your dreams and if you do happen to fail, big deal! Congratulations, you've found one sure-fire way that won't work and you're closer to finding what will work.

A legacy of winning requires a new way of thinking! Let's look at six steps you must master in order to be successful – in anything.

1. **Focus On What You Want:** The Law of Attraction states that whatever you focus your attention on you will attract more of – good or bad. Focus on what you want and you will magnetize it to you. Focus on what you don't want and, likewise, you will pull it right into your reality!

2. **Surround Yourself With Successful People:** Find people who have achieved what you want to achieve and hang out with them. You are the average of the five people you spend the most time with. Take an

honest look at who you associate with the most. What do you talk about? Do you mastermind amazing possibilities for your lives or do you have a weekly gripe session, focusing on everything that is wrong in your lives? Dare to empower yourself by surrounding yourself with successful people. If you're looking to be a better parent, find great parents of whom you can ask questions. If you're looking to create a bigger bank account, find successful entrepreneurs to seek advice from. If you are looking to grow your business, find a successful business person to mastermind with.

3. **Act As If:** Be the leader! Act like the person you desire to be. Act like the person who already possesses what you want.

4. **Be Teachable:** Always be open to learning new things. There is always more to learn – no matter how much of an expert you may be on a particular subject. There is always someone out there who knows more than you. Be willing to listen and think about issues from different perspectives.

5. **Have an "Attitude of Gratitude":** All successful people understand the power of gratitude. If you aren't thankful for what you have right now, then how can you expect to create something even greater? Be grateful for all the wonderful things in your life today, without being complacent.

6. **Live With Intention:** Get clear about what you want in life – what makes your heart sing - your PURPOSE! Then declare it with intention. FEEL IT! Then go after it with everything you have in you.

The Myth of Perfection

When you're in pursuit of a goal - be it a weight goal, a fitness goal, an income goal, a career goal, or whatever – you can often get wrapped up in the idea that you have to be PERFECT in order to achieve it. How many times have you been on a weight control program and found yourself waking from a television-induced coma to find an empty pint of ice cream and a half eaten bag of potato chips staring back at you? Or, you are pursuing a fitness goal and you just can't make yourself get out of bed and drag yourself to the gym one day. You slip and fall off the wagon and then tell yourself, "Well, I've blown it, I may as well quit (or just eat the house and start over next week, etc.)."

I'm sure this will come as no great surprise to you, but I'm here to tell you that if "perfect" is what you are chasing, get ready for lots of disappointment! Perfection simply cannot be achieved on the physical plane – we are imperfect people living in an imperfect world – that's just a fact.

I'm not sure where the idea originated that we can't stumble once or twice (or 50 or 100 times) along the way to our dream life and still get there. What garbage!! What if, every time I got in the cockpit of a plane and made a slight error or accidentally bumped the yoke, I just gave up and quit because I had made a mistake? Easy answer – I'd be dead! The plane would have fallen out of the sky! The difference between success and failure in ANY situation is not whether you are moving in a perfectly straight line to the object of your desire, but whether you pick yourself up, dust yourself off and KEEP GOING when the inevitable stumbles and falls come.

When you realize that you are off course, make a conscious decision in that moment to get back on track – not tomorrow, not next week or next month – but RIGHT NOW!! If you have a career goal and you realize that you haven't been doing the things you need to do to move you toward the next step to your goal, what good does it do to wait until tomorrow – you'll only be further behind!! Take a deep breath as soon as you realize you are off course, close your eyes and see yourself in your mind's eye as already having achieved what you are going after and then, as soon as you open your eyes, take a positive step toward it. If you are, for example, in sales and you realize that you have been spending too much time in the office shuffling piles of paper, rather than out in the world meeting with prospects, don't wait to fix the problem! Pick up the phone and call people and make some sales appointments. Then commit to being in front of a live body each morning by 9:00am and asking them to buy whatever it is that you sell. The point is to break the failure mindset as soon as you realize it's there and move into positive action.

Persistence: It's Not What You Think It Is

So the point is to be persistent, right? Every self-help book and success book I've ever read points to persistence as a key ingredient in the recipe of success. Persistence is the quality of never giving up when we encounter challenges - of holding on to our dream - of refusing to be discouraged no matter what the odds, no matter what happens.

When you read the life stories of very successful people, they will often tell you about all the hardships they encountered along the way. They will tell you about the discouragement they occasionally felt when they encountered failure, and about all the people who laughed at them along the way. Then they will tell you that the reason they are successful today is because they were persistent; they persevered in chasing their dream, no matter what happened.

But there's a catch!! There are a lot of incredibly persistent people in this world who are not successful. Persistence is absolutely key to your success, but it will only work in the presence of a clearly defined goal and a daily plan to move toward that goal.

Successful people step back to evaluate the results all along the way, after every step they take, to see if the results they are getting are the results they want. If they aren't getting the results they want, then they change the next steps they take.

Successful people have incredible persistence, but they are only persistent about holding on to their vision. They are never persistent (or locked into) the method they use to get to their goal. All along the way, the successful person is prepared to be very flexible and experiment to see what techniques and strategies work best to get where they want to go.

Why is it that so many successful people leave out this important detail when they tell the secrets to their success? Why do they so often neglect to mention that if a strategy wasn't working, they abandoned it quickly and moved on to another strategy? I choose to believe that it's because they assume it's very obvious to everyone already. They assume that everyone already knows that you test each step of what you are doing to see whether it's working or not. If it's not working, you change it. You keep trying new approaches until you find something that DOES work, that moves you closer to the result you want.

Let's look at the example of Thomas Edison who kept trying to produce an electrical light bulb even after ten thousand failed attempts. Thomas Edison was persistent in believing in his goal, but he was not at all persistent in the way he tried to achieve it. Thomas Edison did not repeat the same experiment over and over again ten thousand times trying to get a different result. Rather, he adjusted his experiments each time until he finally found what DID work.

Remember this crucial difference the next time someone tries to tell you that persistence is the key to success. Without taking some time to evaluate whether or not what you do is actually working, you can be persistent for years, and not achieve the goals you want.

> When I started my business back in 2008, my goal was to be financially independent to the point that I could do what I wanted, when I wanted. Although my green building consulting practice was generating a decent income, that income was completely dependent on my time – no work, no income. So I held tight to my goal (financial independence), but started examining "out of the box" methods for attaining it. I tried new things. I changed the direction and focus of the company. I brought people into the business with me. I have done that every step of the way – I held the vision but adjusted the tactics to achieve it, always studying what was working and what wasn't. I had the courage to discontinue those programs that weren't working and press forward and expand those that were. Step by step I moved toward my goal.

SHELLSHOCKED - DEALING WITH DISAPPOINTMENT

I'm not telling you anything new when I say that there are going to be times in your life when things just don't go your way and you are going to have to deal with disappointment. It stinks, but it happens and it's just part of the deal. What matters is how you respond to the disappointment. As I write this book, the 2012 presidential elections have just passed in the United States, so I'll use that event to illustrate my point. I have two friends who were engaged in the political process – they each had "their guy" and were really rooting for him to win the election. On Wednesday morning they both woke up to find that, although the election had been a close one, their candidate lost. Both friends were disappointed, but their responses were very different.

One friend, I'll call her "Beth," got angry. She became very upset – her whole physical demeanor was depressed. She posted ugly things on social media and told everyone she came in contact with that the election must have been rigged. She was in a terrible vibration and everyone who came into contact with her could "feel" her dark mood.

My other friend, I'll call her "Jane," saw the election results and was also disappointed; however, she allowed her disappointment to wash over her; she acknowledged it and then she let it go. She refused to allow outside circumstances to ruin an otherwise wonderful day.

Who do you think went on to create success in their life? "Jane" did, of course. We become what we think about most of the time. "Beth" attracted all kinds of negative experiences into her life because she refused to break out of her disappointment. "Jane" had a great day and a great week and so on because she realized that her attitude was crucial to her success.

The funny thing is that "Beth" and "Jane" are really the same person – my partner, Angie – but they might as well be two completely different people. "Beth" was Angie back in 2008. "Jane" was Angie last week. Before Angie knew anything about the material you are learning in this book, she *reacted* to disappointment and,

the more passionate her reaction, the more negativity she pulled into her life. By the time we met in 2010, Angie's reactionary nature had attracted a mountain of debt, a failed marriage, a weight problem, health issues, a dead-end job that she hated and more; however, with awareness, she was able to change the way she dealt with disappointment. Now, when faced with a setback, Angie asks herself a series of questions:

1. Is there anything I can do to change the outcome?
2. Will I or anyone else be served by letting my disappointment consume me?
3. Do I need to apologize to anyone for what happened (did my actions infringe upon the rights of others or hurt anyone)?
4. How can I turn a negative into a positive?

If the answer to any of the first three questions is "yes" then she takes appropriate action. If she answers "No" to questions 1-3, she then proceeds to #4, flips the disappointment on its ear and goes about her day. In the case of last week's election, there was nothing she could do about the outcome, no one would be served by wallowing in her disappointment, and she hadn't wronged anyone – no apologies needed. So she turned the event into a positive affirmation – "I am so happy and grateful that I live in a country where the people have the opportunity to choose their leaders in a free and open process."

When disappointment strikes – and it will – take a moment to breathe because, if your disappointment is strong enough, your inclination will be to react – to lash out, to express your frustration,

REMARKABLE COURAGE

to blame, justify or complain (true signs of poverty consciousness). Instead, respond to the situation – ask yourself those four questions and then decide what action you can take that will make a positive difference (the mark of prosperity consciousness).

OFF BALANCE ON PURPOSE

So many of my clients SAY that they are in pursuit of "balance" in their lives – they want their company to be #1 in its industry, stratospheric revenue/profitability, a top notch quality product and fantastic customer service. Personally, they may strive for a 7-figure income, the dream house, the dream car, the perfect relationship with their spouse and/or their kids, to be at their ideal weight and to live in a healthy body, and on and on – they want it all and they want it now. Well, I am all for wanting it all – I get that – but there's something critically important that everyone reading this book needs to understand right now. If a balanced life is what you are striving for, then you can certainly have it, but it will be a life of balanced mediocrity.

You see, you have a certain amount of energy available to give each and every day. You cannot give more than 100%, right? The more energy you focus on a given area of your life, the faster and more profoundly that area will begin to change. Say your goal is to increase your company's revenue by a factor of ten this coming year. If you and your team focus all your energy on that goal and firmly ground everything you do in the four pillars of success - discipline, accountability, standards and systems - then you can absolutely reach that goal, but if you have multiple goals – increase revenue by ten times, introduce eight new products during the year, revolutionize your inventory control system, etc. – you are going to have to split your energy and focus amongst all of these areas, which means that none of them will receive enough energy to truly quantum leap.

There has to be a *chief aim* – the goal that you want above all else that will receive the majority of your time, attention and focus. That doesn't mean to completely ignore everything else – there is certainly more to a business than revenue (and more to your personal life than your income or the car you drive). You have to devote the majority of your energy to your chief aim, while still focusing enough energy on other areas of your business and your personal life so as to not go backwards in those areas. If you want to quantum leap in one area, then you have to give just enough energy to everything else to move ahead incrementally.

So, living a "balanced" life is a myth – if you are striving for a quantum leap in your results in a certain area, you need to be purposefully unbalanced. Then, when you achieve your huge increase in results in that area, you can redefine your chief aim and redirect the bulk of your energy to another area.

The Common Denominator of Success

Once in a while one of my clients will ask me how it is so effortless for me to create the success I desire in my life. I always laugh, because there is nothing effortless about it – I work my butt off! Plus, as anyone who has tried to continually flip their mindset when Mr. X starts his incessant yammering knows, staying positive and really THINKING is hard work – exhausting work – it takes courage, guts and determination to tell Mr. X to go to hell and then change your attitude in spite of the fact that you're scared to death.

REMARKABLE COURAGE

Anyway, back to the question, I think I have an easier time of it than the average person because of two things:

1. **I have the discipline and the courage to do whatever it takes; once I make a decision to do something or have something, I don't stop until I achieve it. I make decisions quickly, and I rarely change them without a truly compelling reason; and**

2. **I have formed the habit of doing things that most people don't like to do.**

Back in 1940, an insurance company executive named Alfred E. N. Gray delivered a speech at the National Association of Life Underwriters annual convention, and it has become a timeless piece of literature for people in the insurance industry, although Gray's philosophy certainly carries across all industries and all walks of life. Gray talks about his quest to learn the secret to success and how, through a great deal of research, it all boiled down to one thing – the common denominator of success – which was that every person who has achieved considerable success in their business or in their life *formed the habit of doing things that failure don't like to do.*

I think I unconsciously did this as I was growing up and moving through my career. As an example, I'm a big list maker. I always have a continually running list of things I need to do, and, when it comes to choosing what to do next – what items to put on my Daily Commitment Sheet – I pick the thing that I least want to do, just so I can get it out of the way and be done with it. I don't think that is what most people do – I think most people pick the thing they MOST want to do as their next task. Another example is that

I would much rather pick up the phone and call someone to get an answer immediately than wait around for someone to return an email. In this day and age, I think there are a lot of people who rely on texting and private messaging on Facebook and email as their primary modes of connecting with people. My advice? Pick up the PHONE and TALK to people!

Set yourself apart – have the courage to be the kind of person who leads the field, who has formed the habit of doing things most people don't like to do.

The Law of Averages

You've no doubt heard the old adage "Opposites attract," right? I contend that this is not so – I would argue instead that like attracts like. If you put a drop of oil in a glass of water and stir the liquid vigorously, the oil will immediately separate from the water; however, if you put two drops of water on a table top and nudge one close to the other to the point where they touch, the two water droplets will combine into one larger drop of water. I believe that something similar happens with people. I absolutely believe that you are the average of the five people you spend the most time with.

Look at your income, look at your relationships, look at your career trajectory – then examine the same aspects of the lives of the people you surround yourself with. You will find that some are in better shape than you are and some are worse off, but at the end of the day YOUR situation approximates the average of those five people's situations. Interesting, isn't it? The same thing holds for your children. Who are THEY spending the most time with?

If you want to achieve something in your life that is beyond anything you have done before (a real, quantum leap type of goal) and really change some aspect of your life in a huge way, you will find that your averages have to change as well. Does that mean that you need to cut off all contact with everyone in your current circle of friends who doesn't measure up to your goal? Of course not!! That would be ridiculous.

What I want to make you aware of is that you should not be surprised if, as you move toward your goal, your circle of friends begins to change. Old friends may fall away, while new people show up along your path. These new friends will likely be more in alignment with the goal you are moving toward – the Law of Attraction is at work here.

I can personally attest to this fact. When I started studying this material I had a close circle of friends and we got together socially often. The more I studied, the more my own attitude began to change and suddenly I wasn't enjoying the visits with them as much (they usually consisted of lengthy "pity parties" where one or all complained about all the bad stuff in their lives). Over time, I stopped issuing or accepting invitations to get together with them. Remember the crab pot story? I found that my friends would get really mad at me when I wouldn't participate and would get downright hostile when I attempted to use my new "everything happens for a reason" outlook on life; but I attracted NEW friends whose attitudes were much more in alignment with my own. I am still the average of the five people I spent the most time with, but it is a "much higher" average.

Think about where you are going in your life and who you are spending the majority of your time with. Look back and see if you can identify examples in your own life where this law of averages has played out. It is so important to surround yourself with like-minded people as you pursue a new goal. They will support you in your pursuit, become amazing masterminding partners and offer a creative sounding board for problem solving. You ARE the average of the five people you spend the most time with – choose wisely!

Tool: The Gratitude List

Every success you achieve in life will be short-lived and fleeting without maintaining an attitude of gratitude for what you have received. Everything that comes to us is a result of certain universal, non-physical laws that are even more powerful and absolute than the physical laws (ex: the law of gravity) that govern our world.

It is said that if you visualize your heart's desires and hold them on the screen of your mind with your will and then back your desire with faith and expectancy, then that which you desire cannot fail to manifest in your life at the appropriate time through the harmonious interworkings of the Law of Attraction.

Gratitude and faith are intimately linked – gratitude is the natural result of faith. Gratitude is an attitude that hooks us up to our source of supply; and the more grateful you are, the closer you become to your maker, to the architect of the universe, to the spiritual core of your being.

The thing is, it's so easy to ask for help when times are tough, when we need guidance or support, but how often do we stop and truly express our heartfelt gratitude for all the wonderful things that have been placed in our life when things are going well?

So, how do you get yourself hooked up to your source of supply and maintain this attitude of gratitude? The best way I know is by creating a "Gratitude List" every day. It is a fantastic way to start each day in a very positive vibration.

Here's the idea: First, you list 10 things that you are profoundly grateful for – it could be your spouse, your kids, your friends, your pets, the perfect body that is on its way to you in the next year – that's right, you can absolutely be grateful for things that haven't even manifested in your life yet!! Then, just sit quietly and think about those things you wrote – just for a couple of minutes. The power in this exercise can be amplified even further if you create your "gratitude list" right before you imagineer for the day. The gratitude list puts you in the right frame of mind to get the most out of your 30 minutes of Imagineering - you may be surprised by what happens!

ABOUT DEB CHESLOW

As a former Air Force Instructor Pilot who taught airmen to fly advanced supersonic jets and a 3rd Degree Black Belt in Karate, Deb Cheslow demonstrates how to reach goals that most people dream of yet few ever achieve - she gets RESULTS THAT COUNT! Cheslow exemplifies the power of living a courageous life and accomplishing what are generally perceived to be impossible objectives. She shares a systemized strategy for success focusing on four key foundational pillars – discipline, accountability, standards and systems.

Deb is not your typical motivational speaker; she over-delivers with motivation backed by sustainable results. Her entertaining and engaging style, packed with powerful ideas, leaves audiences not only motivated to reach their goals, but also equipped with the tools they need to get the job done. Deb teaches people how to bridge the gap between "information" and "action."

DEB CHESLOW

Two-time best-selling author, speaker, trainer and peak performance strategist, Deb Cheslow, considers it her mission to spread the message that a life of joy and abundance is attainable for anyone. Deb is known for her no-nonsense, direct approach. She believes audiences want, expect and deserve their speaker to be up front and honest about what works and what does not work. She guides companies worldwide in bridging the gap between the information they already possess and the actions they take on that knowledge.

Deb Cheslow lives in Ponce Inlet, Fla., with her family. She has co-authored two bestselling books, *The Simple Success Solution* and *Release – The Simple Success Solution for Real and Permanent Weight Loss*. She is also co-author of *Overcome Dysthymia – Break Free and Create a Life You Love*. Deb has a passion for the martial arts, endurance cycling, health and wellness and weightlifting.

ABOUT DEB CHESLOW CONSULTING

Deb Cheslow Consulting shares a systemized strategy for success based on four foundational pillars – Discipline, Accountability, Standards and Systems. These are strategies that have been consistently used by the Air Force since its inception to create phenomenal results – a system that is easily duplicated for teams, organizations and corporations who seek a quantum leap in their results.

Deb Cheslow Consulting's corporate speaking and training services are transformational and even a simple telephone consultation can be a game changer. Deb Cheslow's unique gift is the ability to see the big picture, identify the strategic holes, and break it all down to simple, actionable steps that can be implemented by every associate the moment they leave the training room.

Every executive wants ground-breaking results for their company, organization, or team. But how do you achieve quantum leaps in results if you keep operating in the same, ineffective manner day after day? In today's business environment it can be easy to lose sight of the forest while focusing on all the trees. Bring the power of Deb Cheslow Consulting's peak performance strategies to your company, organization or team today!

Deb Cheslow understands the unique challenges that managers and executives face today. She understands what it takes to blaze a new trail from first-hand experience. It takes courage to face that inevitable fear of the unknown and to act in spite of that fear. It takes a willingness to put logic aside and "go for it" with everything you have in you. It takes a simple process that everyone in your organization can use to transcend their present results and explode forward. That is what Deb Cheslow Consulting's customized speaking and training services offer you.

Visit us at www.DebCheslow.com or call (386) 308-2155 to schedule Deb Cheslow for your next conference or training event or for a complimentary initial consultation.

Other Books by Deb Cheslow

The Simple Success Solution

The Simple Success Solution Companion Workbook

Overcome Dysthymia – Break Free and Create a Life you Love

Release – The Simple Success Solution for Real and Permanent Weight Loss

www.DebCheslow.com
info@debcheslow.com
(386) 308-2155

www.ingramcontent.com/pod-product-compliance
Lightning Source LLC
Chambersburg PA
CBHW030331230426
43661CB00032B/1373/J